The Encyclopedia of
Pepsi-Cola® Collectibles

by
Bob Stoddard

krause
publications

700 East State Street • Iola, WI 54990-0001
715/445-2214 • FAX: 715/445-4087   www.krause.com

Please call or write for our free catalog of publications. To place an order or obtain a free catalog, or for
editorial comment and further information, please call 715-445-2214.

PEPSI and PEPSI-COLA trademarks were used by permission of PEPSICO INC., Purchase, New York.

Library of Congress Catalog Number 2001096290
ISBN 0-87349-381-8

TABLE OF CONTENTS

ACKNOWLEDGMENTS

This book was made possible with the help of many friends and fellow collectors to whom I give my deepest thanks.

Collections Photographed

Lewis and Chris Carr
Scott and Kim Kinzie
John and Sara Minges
Sterling and Margaret Mann
Craig and Lisa Murray
Rick and Pam Russell
Clifford Rufkahr
Joe and Ann Donofrio
Harold Rosentreter
Dan and Judy Durbin
Dave Ezell and Maggi Pratt
Mark and Ellen Zobrist
Pepsi-Cola Bottling Company of New Haven, Missouri
Gary Metz, Muddy River Trading Company
Steve Rosentreter

Other Contributions

Michael Noll

Editors

Bob Stoddard
Sue Gustin

ABOUT THE AUTHOR

Bob Stoddard is recognized as the leading authority on Pepsi-Cola memorabilia. His interest in collecting first began in 1977 with the purchase of a vintage Pepsi cooler to house an ample supply of Pepsi-Cola. As any true collector can attest, one of anything is never enough. Twenty-five years later, his collection is one of the largest in the world, consisting of more than 3,000 items, including a rare 1909 straw holder valued over $7,000.

In 1983 Stoddard founded the Pepsi-Cola Collectors Club as a way to bring fellow collectors together to exchange information about their collections, and to buy, sell, and trade. Today, the club boasts more than 4,000 members worldwide. In exchanging information with other collectors, it became apparent to Stoddard that there was a need for accurate, reliable information about Pepsi-Cola memorabilia. Price guides that did exist were incomplete and contained many errors regarding dating and nomenclature. He decided to publish a book that would clear up inaccuracies and misinformation.

With the publication of *Introduction to Pepsi Collecting*, Stoddard realized that he had a full-time job in the promotion of Pepsi collectibles. He quit his job in marketing in 1991, and formed Double Dot Enterprises (Double Dot: a term referring to older Pepsi-Cola trademark logos). His reputation for thorough research, and keen knowledge of antique advertising memorabilia soon led to a consulting agreement with the Pepsi-Cola Company. For the past fifteen years, he has traveled throughout the country displaying his collection at Pepsi-Cola sponsored functions. During this time he has written additional books on Pepsi. In 1996, *The Complete Guide To Pepsi-Cola Collectibles* was released, followed by *Pepsi: 100 Years* in 1997, and *Pepsi Now and Then* in 1999.

Most recently, Stoddard was featured as a leading expert on Pepsi-Cola history in *The Cola Wars*, a historical documentary on the History Channel. He has also served as historical consultant for movies such as Oliver Stone's *Nixon*, and numerous television and radio shows to recount the history of the Pepsi-Cola Company. Signs and bottles from his collection have been featured in television shows and commercials. Additionally, he has compiled collections for various theme restaurants, including Mel's Diner at Universal Studios, Hollywood, California.

ABOUT PEPSI COLLECTING

Pepsi-Cola memorabilia collectors are among the most dedicated of all collectors. Collecting Pepsi-Cola artifacts is both difficult and challenging. This is due in great part to the turbulent beginning experienced by the Pepsi-Cola Company. Financial difficulties, combined with political and economic conditions, made Pepsi-Cola's first years more about survival than about selling soft drinks. This resulted in limited amounts of Pepsi-Cola advertising materials produced. With two bankruptcies and several moves, much of the material that was produced was either destroyed or lost. This includes most of the records of what was made. Unlike other collectibles, no one can say for certain what Pepsi memorabilia exists. This is truly the most exciting part of being a Pepsi collector. No one knows for certain what's out there. Every time you look for Pepsi stuff, you have a chance of finding something that no collector has ever seen before. The scarcity of Pepsi collectibles results in a higher value of older Pepsi memorabilia.

Within the world of Pepsi collecting, there are many sub-categories. One can specialize in bottles, cans, toys, signs, crowns (bottle caps), or paper. Within these categories, some collectors decide to specialize in a sub-category. For example, a bottle collector may specialize in commemorative bottles. The possibilities are endless of how you can make Pepsi collecting fit your own interest.

If you are just getting started, it is important for you to observe some guidelines. Most importantly, you should only buy what you like. Deal only with reputable antique dealers who will guarantee the authenticity of what they are selling in writing. Keep good records of what you buy. In order to ensure that Pepsi collecting will always be fun for you, do not spend more than you can afford.

Meeting other collectors makes the hobby so much more interesting. One of the best ways to do that is through participation in the Pepsi-Cola Collectors Club. This gives you an opportunity to meet other collectors and exchange information.

As a Pepsi collector, you are collecting the artifacts of the Pepsi-Cola Company. In some cases, these artifacts are irreplaceable pieces of Pepsi history, and it is important that you care for them properly. Proper framing of cardboard signs and paper documents will not only aid in preservation, but also add to their beauty. In the long run, taking good care of your Pepsi collection will only add to its value.

One of the most frequently asked questions about Pepsi collecting is "where can I find Pepsi-Cola memorabilia?" The answer is: Everywhere — at yard sales, flea markets, antique stores, and auctions. You can even find Pepsi stuff in your local grocery store. At times, old signs get left in a corner or hidden away — you never know. Ultimately, the best place to enrich your Pepsi collection is Pepsi Fest, an annual event hosted by the Pepsi-Cola Collectors Club.

PREFACE

Knowledge about what you are collecting is an important part of the enjoyment of Pepsi collecting. In this, my third book on Pepsi collectibles, the content is expanded to include more information about the original usage and history of Pepsi memorabilia. The field of advertising memorabilia is an exciting one, but can be fraught with pitfalls concerning the price, grading, rarity, and dating of an item. With this book, I hope to help the novice, as well as the experienced collector, in the appraisal and acquisition of Pepsi memorabilia.

In my last Pepsi collecting book, I adopted a rarity scale that has become a standard among Pepsi collectors. To many collectors, the scarcity of an item can be more important than its price. A rare item that is overpriced may be a justifiable purchase. On the other hand, an overpriced, common item could be purchased at another time and perhaps at a better price. The rarity scale ranges from "A" to "E." "A" items are the most common because they were widely produced, generally newer, and inexpensive. "E" items are extremely rare, with only a few known in existence. Most items, you will find, range between the two extremes. This scale should be a factor in what you are willing to pay for a Pepsi-Cola collectible.

In books on collectibles, pricing is always the most controversial aspect. It is necessary that collectors be able to attach a reasonable value to the pieces they own, as well as those they are interested in buying. As with any collectible, it is difficult to do this. Prices rise and fall solely on the basis of supply and demand. I have tried to be as consistent as possible in establishing a hierarchical price structure that values each piece in relation to other pieces of the same age and rarity. Ultimately, the prices in this book should be a *guide*. Prices change continuously, both rising and falling. The prices given in this book assume that the item is in near mint condition. For any condition less than near mint, the price should be adjusted accordingly.

Grading is an important aspect of pricing. Condition is everything. In valuing advertising collectibles, the visibility of the logo, trademark, etc. is vitally important in establishing price. Buyers should also be aware that missing parts, mechanical dysfunction, and retouching all detract from the value of a piece. Sizes are included to give the reader a perspective of dimension. In most cases, they are rounded to whole numbers for simplicity, and are not meant to be used for purposes of authentication.

Dating Pepsi memorabilia is not an exact science. As much as possible, dates have been derived from Pepsi-Cola corporate documents and paper pieces with original dates. Putting these facts together with what we know about the history of Pepsi advertising (changes in colors, bottle styles, slogans) gives us approximate dates of usage. All dates used in this book are based on first known usage. In other words, an advertising sign may have been produced by Pepsi-Cola for several years, but the dates in this book only reflect when the sign was first issued. In some cases, an individual bottler may have used a trademark or bottle style beyond the period of time authorized by the Pepsi-Cola Company. This is rarely done today, but in the 1930s, 1940s, and 1950s, this was a common practice. The information provided in this book can be useful to accurately date your Pepsi memorabilia.

Appraising advertising memorabilia is often a subjective task, but one that is critical to the informed purchase of a collectible. This book is a guide in making that task easier for Pepsi collectors. To be a successful Pepsi collector, you have to become your own expert.

REFERENCE GUIDE

Two of the most important factors in determining the value of a Pepsi collectible are condition and rarity. No matter how rare or old something is, if it is faded, cracked, or missing pieces, the value will be negatively affected. Remember, you are buying these items to display. If most of the image is gone, you cannot really enjoy the item. If you come across a very rare piece, you can pay a little more than you thought you would because of its scarcity. Remember, supply and demand is an important part in determining value. The bottom line is that a rare piece in excellent condition will command top dollar.

This cardboard sign, though rare, is in terrible shape, with cracks and missing pieces. You should only buy a piece in this condition if it is inexpensive.

This cardboard sign is rare and in mint condition. Overpaying for a sign like this is very acceptable.

This metal carrier is very common. You should only buy common items in good condition, and pay book value or less. On the scarcity scale, this is an "A" - very common.

Although the condition of this cardboard sign isn't perfect, it is good enough, considering the rarity. On the scarcity scale, this is an E+ - very rare.

A BRIEF HISTORY OF THE PEPSI-COLA COMPANY

Once upon a time, soft drinks were created in the back room of local drug stores. The druggist would try various mixtures of new and exotic ingredients. Most of these new drinks never gained more than local fame, but a few went on to become household names. Pepsi-Cola is one of those drinks that traces its roots back to the corner drugstore. In 1898, Caleb Bradham, of New Bern, North Carolina, invented it.

The Pepsi story is typical of most soft drinks. The local druggist, Bradham, experimenting with different formulas, came up with one that was very popular with the local clientele. The drink was initially nicknamed "Brad's Drink," after the inventor. Soon Bradham believed his creation needed a more marketable name. After all, his drink was developed not only as refreshment, but also as a means to invigorate a tired soul. It is believed that the name Pepsi-Cola is derived from a combination of the words pepsin and cola. Bradham believed that his new drink aided digestion similar to the way the pepsin enzyme does. However, Pepsi never contained pepsin. "Cola" represents the refreshing and invigorating qualities of the drink. By 1900, Pepsi-Cola had become so popular, that Bradham started the Pepsi-Cola Company. At first, the Pepsi-Cola Company simply sold Pepsi-Cola syrup to drug stores in eastern North Carolina.

By 1905, demand for Pepsi-Cola had increased so much that Bradham decided it was time to offer Pepsi-Cola for sale in bottles. To facilitate the sale of Pepsi-Cola in bottles, Bradham issued the first of many franchise agreements. Soon the name of Pepsi-Cola was known throughout the southeastern United States. As 1910 approached, there were nearly 240 Pepsi-Cola bottling franchises. This resulted in the need for the first Pepsi-Cola bottler's convention, which was held in 1910.

One of the reasons for Pepsi-Cola's popularity, besides the good taste, was that it was pure. Unlike many of the other popular drinks of the day, Pepsi did not contain any harmful ingredients. Some of Pepsi's competitors used narcotics and other dangerous substances in their formulas. In 1906, the United States government enacted the Pure Food and Drug Act, which required food and drug companies to remove dangerous ingredients from their products. Pepsi was not required to change their already pure formula. As a result of this act, in 1907, Pepsi began using "pure, food drink" as part of their advertisement.

Bradham was very pleased with this designation, because it was his desire to create a drink that would have no harmful effects. The original Pepsi-Cola formula did not even contain caffeine. Because Pepsi was so healthy for people, it was even advertised as a drink that was safe for children. It was suggested in advertising that Pepsi-Cola would help children grow up healthy.

Sales were now exceeding Bradham's wildest expectations. A new home office was built in 1908. Tens of thousands of dollars were spent promoting Pepsi-Cola. Everything from tip trays to hand fans were given out as advertising premiums to Pepsi-Cola customers. An advertising agency was employed to improve Pepsi advertising. One of their first efforts was to hire famed racecar driver, Barney Oldfield, to endorse Pepsi-Cola.

Success continued for Bradham and Pepsi-Cola between 1910 and 1915. The net income for the Pepsi-Cola Company in 1915 was $31,346. Pepsi-Cola was now being sold in Virginia, North Carolina, South Carolina, Georgia, Florida, Alabama, and Tennessee. At the same time, Bradham was making plans to sell Pepsi-Cola throughout the rest of the United States.

Unfortunately, times were about to get tough for Pepsi-Cola. On June 28th, 1914, Archduke Francis Ferdinand was assassinated in the city of Sarajevo, Bosnia, triggering World War I. Within a few short years, the effects of the war reached New Bern, North Carolina, and Pepsi-Cola. Sugar shortages and price controls decimated the profits of the Pepsi-Cola Company.

Initially, Bradham's biggest problem was finding enough sugar to manufacture Pepsi-Cola syrup. At times, he was forced to use sugar substitutes, which in some cases altered the good taste of Pepsi-Cola.

Eventually, this sub-standard Pepsi-Cola would affect the sales substantially. After the conclusion of the war, price controls were lifted, resulting in extremely high sugar prices. The cost of sugar soared from 3 cents per pound, to over 28 cents per pound. With the price of soft drinks well established at 5 cents a bottle or glass, Pepsi had no choice but to absorb the additional cost of sugar. Concerned that the price of sugar would continue to rise, Bradham was forced to purchase a large quantity of sugar at 28 cents per pound. Soon after this purchase, the bottom fell out of the sugar market, with prices tumbling to a pre-war low. This was the final straw that would eventually lead to the bankruptcy of the Pepsi-Cola Company.

Several attempts were made to revive the financially starved Pepsi-Cola Company. One such attempt was made to dissolve the old Pepsi-Cola Company and incorporate a new Pepsi-Cola Company with a new stock offering. This was too little, too late. On May 31, 1923, the Pepsi-Cola Company was certified bankrupt. The assets of the company were eventually sold to the Craven Holding Corporation for $35,000.

Meanwhile, in Richmond, Virginia, the Old Dominion Beverage Company was looking for a replacement for Taka-Kola. The Coca-Cola Company had challenged the Taka-Kola trademark in court. The court ruled in favor of the Coca-Cola Company, forcing the Taka-Kola Company to operate without a cola drink. The owners of the Old Dominion Company met with the Craven Holding Company, and decided that Pepsi-Cola would be a suitable replacement for Taka-Kola. Rather than just sell the Pepsi-Cola formula to Old Dominion, they decided to merge the two companies together to create the Pepsi-Cola Corporation of Richmond, Virginia.

From the beginning, the new Pepsi-Cola Corporation was undercapitalized, causing a succession of financial problems. With these problems came changes within management and investors. By 1928, the Pepsi-Cola Corporation was reorganized into a new company named the National Pepsi-Cola Corporation. The National Pepsi-Cola Corporation tried desperately to regain the former success of Pepsi-Cola. They created new advertising, introduced a new bottle design, and made an all-out effort to recruit new bottlers. Unfortunately, their timing was terrible. On October 29th, 1929, the stock market in the United States crashed. This crash eventually led to the Great Depression, resulting in a serious economic downturn. By May of 1931, Pepsi-Cola was once again bankrupt.

In New York, Charles Guth, president of Loft Candy, was in a bitter dispute with Coca-Cola over the wholesale price of Coca-Cola syrup. Loft operated over 130 soda fountains in the greater New York area. Guth believed that with that kind of volume, Loft deserved better pricing. Coca-Cola believed that Guth had no choice but to buy their syrup, and refused to offer any discount. Guth, unaccustomed to being told no, decided to replace Coca-Cola at his soda fountains. Word reached Guth that the trademark and formula for Pepsi-Cola was being sold in a bankruptcy sale. He decided that Pepsi-Cola would make the perfect soft drink for Loft soda fountains. In 1931, Guth purchased the trademark and formula for the sum of $9,600, thus making Loft the new parent company of Pepsi-Cola.

After refinement of the Pepsi-Cola formula at the Loft laboratories, Pepsi-Cola was ready for distribution to the soda fountains. Despite advertising and a competitive price, New York was not ready for this drink from North Carolina. After several years of struggling, there was no significant increase in sales of Pepsi-Cola at the Loft Drug stores. After several attempts to increase sales, Guth decided to sell Pepsi-Cola in a fancy 12-ounce bottle for ten cents. Pepsi's prospects went from bad to worse. With their backs to the wall, it was time for a daring move. The price of Pepsi-Cola was reduced from 10 cents a bottle to 5 cents for a 12-ounce bottle. With most of the competition selling a 6-ounce bottle for a nickel, this was a bargain that New Yorkers could not pass up. Overnight, Pepsi-Cola became an instant success.

Guth realized he had a winner and moved quickly to set up bottling operations across America. With just a handful of bottlers in 1934, the number grew to 315 Pepsi-Cola bottlers in 1939. Once again, Pepsi-Cola was on the rise, surpassing all previous successes. Unfortunately, as Pepsi-Cola's prospects increased, Loft Candy fortunes took a severe downturn. Believing that Pepsi-Cola had more potential than Loft, Guth left the candy company, taking Pepsi-Cola with him. This began a multi-year court battle between Loft and Guth over the legal rights to Pepsi-Cola. In 1939, Loft prevailed. Pepsi-Cola was once again part of Loft. Shortly thereafter, Loft changed its name to Pepsi-Cola, and liquidated all of the assets of the candy business. This created the new Pepsi-Cola Company.

During the court battles with Guth, Loft had run out of money. In desperate need of cash, they turned to Phoenix securities, a firm that specialized in helping companies on the verge of going out of business. In exchange for much needed cash, Phoenix received a percentage of the Loft Company, and a seat on the board of directors. Phoenix selected Walter Mack to become part of the Loft board. In 1939, Walter Mack was made the president of the Pepsi-Cola Company. Mack soon took total control of Pepsi-Cola—everything from production to advertising. Aware of the importance of advertising in the soft drink business, Mack made an all-out effort to improve Pepsi-Cola advertising. The three most important promotions at this time were the adoption of the Pepsi-Cola jingle to be used in all Pepsi advertising, the creation of Pepsi and Pete, the Pepsi-Cola Cops, and skywriting. Pepsi-Cola was the first to use skywriting as an advertising medium. This new advertising campaign helped to increase Pepsi sales and make consumers more aware of the big nickel drink. The future could not have looked better for Pepsi-Cola. Sadly, a new problem was on the horizon—World War II.

World War II brought new challenges for Pepsi-Cola. Sugar, a key ingredient in Pepsi-Cola, was now being rationed. The rationing rules favored companies that had been in business for a long time. Most Pepsi bottlers were just getting started. Added to this problem were gasoline rationing, material shortages, and manpower shortages. Many Pepsi bottlers left their businesses to enlist in the military. Mack was not the type of person that easily gave up. He went about trying to find ways to solve each of these problems. One of his most interesting solutions was "El Masco," sugar syrup designed to circumvent the sugar importation rules of World War II. This, along with many other ingenious solutions to problems kept the bottlers in operation. With hard work and luck, Pepsi survived World War II.

Pepsi-Cola management believed that the end of the war cleared the way for Pepsi to once again begin its quest to becoming the number one cola drink. Post-war inflation, however, had a devastating effect on this goal. Too many dollars and too few products caused escalating prices. Unfortunately, Pepsi-Cola had advertised their nickel drink so much, that they were forced to try to hold the price at 5 cents. With their competitor selling a 6-ounce bottle for 5 cents, Pepsi's profit margin had always been thin. Now that margin was gone. In order to survive, something had to be done. Some bottlers raised their price from 5 cents to 6 cents. Other bottlers switched to a 10-ounce bottle for 5 cents. All efforts to regain Pepsi's previous success were unfruitful. By 1950, Pepsi-Cola was once again on the brink of bankruptcy.

Mack had fought hard to maintain the 5-cent price of Pepsi. Many bottlers resented this, because the bargain price came at the cost of their profits. The conflict between Mack and the bottlers led to the board of directors deciding to make a change in the leadership. In 1951, Mack was elevated to chairman of the board, and Alfred Steele became the new president of the Pepsi-Cola Company. Steele had been a vice-president with the Coca-Cola Company. Known for his leadership and showmanship qualities, Steele's mission was to resurrect Pepsi once again.

Steele's first goal was to make Pepsi-Cola a professional company. He felt that Pepsi lacked a consistent image nationwide. In many cases, the taste changed from region to region. He was determined to have all the bottlers use the same advertising, get the drivers to wear the same uniform, and most importantly, get the same Pepsi taste from one city to the next.

His biggest challenge was the image of Pepsi-Cola. The resurgence of Pepsi began during the Great Depression. The 12-ounce bottle for 5 cents became known as the bargain drink. In the post war prosperity of America, a bargain drink was not as desirable as it had been during less prosperous times. Additionally, American taste had changed. Excessively sweet drinks became less popular. To meet these challenges, Steele had Pepsi-Cola reformulated to contain less sugar. The advertising campaign that accompanied this new formula was "Pepsi-Cola, The Light Refreshment." The ad campaign was complete with magazine and billboard ads featuring young, attractive men and women enjoying Pepsi-Cola.

The changes instituted by Steele paid off immediately. By 1955, sales had more than doubled. Once again, Pepsi was back on track. Steele's leadership continued to guide Pepsi-Cola's growth throughout the 1950s. By 1959, sales hit an all time record of 13 million; ten times what it was in 1950. To further improve Pepsi's public image, a new bottle was introduced in 1958. The new "swirl" bottle replaced the bottle Pepsi had used since 1940. Along with the bottle, came a new advertising campaign—"Be Sociable, Have a Pepsi."

In 1959, Steele embarked on a tour to promote Pepsi's new advertising to the bottlers. The stress and exhaustion of this high-powered tour resulted in Steele suffering a fatal heart attack. The man that was responsible for modernizing Pepsi-Cola was suddenly gone, leaving a leadership void that would be difficult to fill. Even today, many of the bottlers still credit Al Steele with turning Pepsi-Cola around and making it a modern soft drink company.

One of Steele's most important accomplishments was to change the focus of Pepsi advertising from the product to image; in other words, he advocated selling the "sizzle," not the steak. During the 1960s, advertising was designed to enhance the image of Pepsi, including the highly successful "Pepsi Generation" campaign. Finally, the image of Pepsi as the bargain drink was eradicated once and for all.

The 1960s saw a major change in the way all companies, including Pepsi, advertised. The growing popularity of television gave advertisers an abundant audience to hear about their products. As the popularity of television increased, so did the advertising rates. Eventually, television spots received the largest share of the Pepsi-Cola advertising budget. This resulted in less money being spent on advertising signage. The golden age of Pepsi point-of-purchase advertising was over.

In 1963, Donald Kendall became president of the Pepsi-Cola Company. Kendall first received prominence within the Pepsi organization in 1959. At that time, he was president of Pepsi International. At a trade expo in Moscow, Kendall had convinced then vice-president Richard Nixon to get the former USSR premiere, Nikita Khrushchev, to visit the Pepsi exhibit at the expo. When Khrushchev stopped to sample Pepsi, all the press photographers snapped pictures. The next day, the headlines around the world read "Khrushchev Gets Sociable." The headlined referred to the advertising slogan "Be Sociable, Have a Pepsi."

While president of the Pepsi-Cola Company, Kendall spearheaded the effort to create Diet Pepsi, and negotiate the purchase of Mountain Dew from Tip Corporation. Despite this, most considered his biggest accomplishment was his successful merger between Frito-Lay and Pepsi-Cola to form PepsiCo in 1965. Finally, Pepsi was established as one of the great American consumer product companies.

Now able to compete on equal footing with the Coca-Cola Company, Pepsi-Cola has earned its way as a legitimate soft drink company. With promotions such as the Pepsi Challenge, Pepsi has, at times, been able to outsell their long-time nemesis. In 1985, Coca-Cola changed their original formula to become more like Pepsi, resulting in Pepsi's declaration that they had won the cola war.

Today, Pepsi-Cola is considered to be a total beverage company, selling everything from Pepsi-Cola to iced tea. The dream of Caleb Bradham, to sell the public a refreshing drink, continues. Pepsi-Cola products are now available in over 186 countries around the world.

Throughout the history of the Pepsi-Cola Company, a number of trademarks were used to represent the cola company. Knowing when each trademark was used is key to identifying the age of Pepsi-Cola memorabilia. Most of the time, this information will help you correctly date your Pepsi-Cola memorabilia. However, there are occasions when this may not be the most accurate way to date your Pepsi items, as trademarks were used at times beyond the date the company started using a new version.

Identified in this section are the major trademark changes. There are numerous minor variations to many Pepsi-Cola trademarks that are not shown here. Overall, this should be an aid in identifying Pepsi memorabilia. There is no way to be 100 percent accurate, but with the use of this chart and the dates slogans were used, you should be very close most of the time.

1898 - This is considered by most to be the first Pepsi-Cola trademark. Unfortunately, there is no evidence that this trademark was ever used by Caleb Bradham. It is alleged that this logo was designed by a local artist. My guess is that this design was the model for the Pepsi trademark that was eventually used.

1903 - Similar to the first logo, this trademark was actually used in a newspaper advertisement in 1903. This logo was the first to incorporate advertising information into the design. Some characteristics were adopted from the 1898 logo, but overall this was a new design.

1906 - This trademark was registered with the United States Patent Office on August 7, 1906. This logo appears to be the 1903 logo, but more streamlined and modernized. We now see a logo that is similar to the double dot script used for most of Pepsi-Cola's first fifty years.

1909 -By this time, the trademark had evolved into a logo that symbolized a modern, professional company. This logo, with minor variations, was used by Pepsi-Cola from 1909 through 1950.

1939 -This is a refinement of the 1909 trademark, with a significant new characteristic. The trademark now features a think blue line around the Pepsi-Cola letters. This line was primarily used in 1939. However, you can find it on some memorabilia in later years.

1940 - This trademark, introduced in 1940, was nicknamed the flag logo for obvious reasons. Essentially, it incorporated the standard script logo into a flag background. It is important to notice that the script logo is balanced by the wave design in the flag. This was the beginning of making the trademark more than just the script logo.

1943 - The flag logo evolved into an oval logo, giving the white wave background a more dynamic look. This is an important transition, because this design would become the genesis of the crown logo.

1945 - The crown logo, taken from the Pepsi-Cola bottle cap, replaced the oval as Pepsi's primary icon. Looking at the center of the bottle cap, you can see remnants of the flag as well as the oval logo. Also, at this time, red, white and blue became the corporate colors of the Pepsi-Cola Company.

1951 - In the 1950s, Pepsi decided to modernize their image. One step in doing this was to give the trademark a face-lift. Therefore, in 1951, Pepsi made one of the biggest changes in their logo since the days of Caleb Bradham. The double dot script was replaced by a sleek, more modern-looking single dot script.

1951 -At the same time, the crown logo was redesigned to incorporate the new single dot script. The new crown trademark tilted slightly to the right, but was definitely the descendant of the 1945 crown. The single dot crown logo became the predominant Pepsi symbol in the 1950s.

1963 - A new decade began with many changes going on in our society. To reflect this new era, the Pepsi logo was once again updated. The image of the crown was less defined, and the familiar Pepsi-Cola script was replaced with block letters.

1965 - The 1963 logo update turned out to be short-lived. By 1965, the trademark was once again changed. The crown part of the logo completely disappeared. Only the wave, first developed in 1943, remained. The emphasis on Pepsi-Cola's name had changed to just "Pepsi."

1971 - In time for Pepsi's 75th anniversary, a new trademark was introduced. The logo featured Pepsi framed by the wave on the top and bottom, with what appears to be bookends on each side. This logo became known as the "bookend" logo. The logo consisted of the red, white, and blue look that Pepsi had first adopted in 1945. Additionally, a lighter shade of blue was included.

1987 - A variation of the bookend logo with new block print. The block print used since 1963 was replaced by a new style- most notably the rounded "E."

1991 - The modified crown logo becomes secondary in the trademark to the block print. The name Pepsi is the featured part of this '90s logo.

1996 - The circle is complete. The crown logo is once again the predominant Pepsi trademark, modernized and named the "globe," but still bearing the essential characteristics that were first created in 1940. If you go back and look at the 1940 flag logo, you can see the roots of the globe logo.

1998 - The globe and the Pepsi-Cola letters are married together, forming a more traditional-looking trademark. The important feature of this trademark is the blue background, which, during the 1990s, became the corporate color of Pepsi-Cola.

PEPSI-COLA ADVERTISING SLOGANS

1903: Exhilarating, Invigorating, Aids Digestion

1907: Original Pure Food Drink

1908: Delicious and Healthful

1915: For All Thirsts - Pepsi-Cola

1919: Pepsi-Cola - It Makes You Scintillate

1920: Drink Pepsi-Cola - It Will Satisfy You

1928: Peps You Up!

1929: Here's Health!

1932: Sparkling, Delicious

1933: It's the Best Cola Drink

1934: Double Size

1934: Refreshing and Healthful

1938: Join the Swing to Pepsi-Cola

1939 Twice as Much for a Nickel

1943: Bigger Drink, Better Taste

1947: It's a Great American Custom

1949: Why Take Less When Pepsi's Best

1950: More Bounce to the Ounce

1954: The Light Refreshment

1958: Be Sociable, Have a Pepsi

1961: Now It's Pepsi for Those Who Think Young

1963: Come Alive! You're in the Pepsi Generation

1967: Taste that Beats the Others Cold. Pepsi Pours It On

1969: You've Got a Lot to Live. Pepsi's Got a Lot to Give

1973: Join the Pepsi People Feelin' Free

1976: Have a Pepsi Day

1979: Catch that Pepsi Spirit

1981: Pepsi's Got Your Taste for Life

1983: Pepsi Now!

1984: The Choice of a New Generation

1992: Gotta Have It

1993: Be Young, Have Fun, Drink Pepsi

1995: Nothing Else is a Pepsi

1997: Generation Next

1999: The Joy of Cola

2001: The Joy of Pepsi

SIGNS

During the first half of the twentieth century, signage was an important part of Pepsi-Cola's advertising program. Before television, advertising signs were key to remind customers to drink Pepsi-Cola. There was a battle to get signs in the most visible locations in every mom and pop grocery store across America. For this reason, a number of different shapes and styles of signs were created, including signs that were to be used exclusively indoors, and others that were to be used outside. Some of these signs were made to fit under windows, and others on screen doors. The main objective was to place signs in strategic locations, where consumers would be sure to notice them. With the advances in technology, and increased competition, signs became more sophisticated. This resulted in everything from neon signs to multi-colored, three-dimensional cardboard signs.

To help make cardboard signs more attractive, Pepsi employed some of the best artists available, including Rolf Armstrong, George Petty, and Zoe Mozert. If you own a Pepsi-Cola memorabilia done by any of these artists, you own a piece of *art*.

For the Pepsi-Cola Company, the years between 1930 and 1960 were the golden years of advertising signage. During this time, Pepsi produced some of their best, and no doubt most collectible advertising signs. This period represents the bulk of Pepsi-Cola advertising signage. If you collect Pepsi-Cola memorabilia, it is more than likely that your collection will include a significant number of items from this era.

We might disagree as to which Pepsi items are best to collect. But, there is no doubt that Pepsi signs offer collectors a great way to decorate their homes. In fact, many of the early Pepsi cardboard signs could be considered works of art. Regardless of your reason for collecting Pepsi signs, you are among the special few that hold a piece of Pepsi-Cola's past.

The signs in this section have been arbitrarily designated into categories. These designations are done for convenience, and have no official standing. Many of these signs could easily fit into two or three different categories. The nomenclature used to identify different styles and types of signs is based on soft drink industry standards.

DIE-CUT

Die-cut refers to using a die during the printing process to cut a sign to a specific shape. Most die-cut cardboard signs have easels attached to the back so they may sit on a counter or be displayed on a wall. These signs are some of the most outstanding point-of-purchase material produced by the Pepsi-Cola Company. Because of their beauty, die-cut Pepsi signs are in high demand, and command premium value.

#0001
1905   E+ $2000
6" x 24"

#0002
1905   E+ $1500
Double Sided   9" Tall

#0003
1928   E $450
Back Bar   8" x 4"

#0004
1936   D+ $750
Easel Back   5" x 16"

#0005
1936   D+ $1200
23" x 26"

#0006
1936   D+ $900
Easel Back   10" x 16"

#0007
1936   D $1000
Easel Back   19" x 15"

#0008
1938   E+ $750
12" x 19"

#0009

1938   E $800

12" x 16"

#0010

1938   E $750

8" x 19"

#0011

1938   E $1200

21" x 25"

#0012

1940   E $850

10" x 13"

#0013

1943   E $300

Display   11" x 17"

#0014

1943   E $450

Double-Sided 11" x 12"

#0015

1943   D+ $250

5" x 8"

#0016

1945   E $850

12" x 18"

#0017

1947   E $700

8" x 18"

#0018

1950   D+ $350

14" x 21"

#0019

1950   D+ $150

11" x 14"

#0020

1954   B+ $85

3-D   17" x 21"

#0021

1954   C+ $75

3-D   14" x 23"

#0022

1954   C $65

13" x 19"

#0023

1954   C+ $65

13" x 19"

#0024

1954   C+ $65

18" x 20"

#0025

1954   C+ $65

12" x 20"

#0026

1954   C+ $65

18" x 20"

#0027

1954   C+ $75

18" x 20"

#0028

1954   C+ $85

18" x 20"

#0029

1960   C+ $75

23" x 25"

#0030

1949   E $750

Easel Back   14" x 26"

#0031

1949   E $750

Easel Back   14" x 26"

#0032

1951   D $400

19" x 21"

#0033

1951   C+ $350

Easel Back   20" x 48"

#0034

1959   C+ $250

Easel Back   34" x 48"

#0035

1959   C+ $150

Easel Back   74" Tall

FIVE GORGEOUS GIRLS

"Five Gorgeous Girls" was the name that was used to identify these five cardboard images. They were introduced in 1949. At that time, the Pepsi bottler paid $2.00 per set for these beautiful cardboard signs. Because of their beauty and rarity, they have become very popular among collectors of antique advertising. It is difficult to find the whole set together, but that is the fun of collecting!

#0036

1949   E- $1000

18" x 23"

#0038

1949   E- $1000

18" x 23"

#0037

1949   E- $1000

18" x 23"

The above picture is from a Pepsi Bottler bulletin depicting how these signs might be displayed.

#0039

1949   E- $1000

14" x 38"

#0040

1949   E- $1000

17" x 38"

#0041

1939   E $500

14" x 18"

#0042

1940   D+ $1500

29" x 40"

#0043

1941   D+ $500

34" x 30"

#0044

1943   E $1500

25" x 33"

#0045

1943   D+ $650

Easel Back   28" x 33"

#0046

1936   D+ $800

10" x 32"

#0047

1948   D+ $400

3-D   28" x 26"

#0048

1950   E $500

20" x 25"

#0049

1951   C+ $350

Easel Back   24" x 25"

#0050

1943   E $500

40" x 22"

#0051

1943   D+ $500

Easel Back   30" x 21"

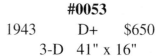

#0052

1943   D $450

21" Dia.

#0053

1943   D+ $650

3-D   41" x 16"

#0054

1943   D $350

21" x 24"

#0055

1943   D+ $600

36" x 38"

#0056

1905   E+ $8500

20" x 34"

#0057

1940   E $2500

Easel Back   66" Tall

#0058

1947   E+ $2500

Easel Back   30" x 68"

#0059

1987   B- $25

Easel Back   72" Tall

#0060
1905   E+ $1500
Paper   11" x17"

#0061
1907   E+ $10000
10" x 12.5"

#0062
1907   E+ $6500
10" x 12.5"

RARE LITHOGRAPHS

Represented on this page are some of the rarest and most sought after Pepsi-Cola collectibles. Created by some of the best illustrators of the time, these signs are classics. Sadly, lithographed cardboard signs, if not kept in optimum conditions, will deteriorate over time. For this reason, only a limited number of these signs survived. If you have have an opportunity to buy one of these signs and can afford it, don't hesitate about the investment.

#0063
1909   E+ $4500
20" x 25"

#0064
1909   E+ $5000
18" x 24"

#0065
1919   D+ $3500
25" x 31"

THREE-DIMENSIONAL SELF-FRAMED

These signs represent some of Pepsi-Cola's finest point of purchase advertising from the 1940s. These beautiful Pepsi girls are surrounded by a three-dimensional cardboard frame that is part of the sign. Because of the fragile construction of these signs, it is rare to find them in good condition. For this reason, it is recommended that if you find any of these signs in good shape, purchase it.

#0066

1940   D+ $1500
Cardboard   24" x 34"

#0067

1943   D+ $1500
Cardboard   24" x 34"

#0068

1943   D+ $1500
Cardboard   24" x 34"

#0069

1943   D+ $1500
Cardboard   24" x 31"

#0070

1943   D+ $1500
Cardboard   24" x 34"

#0071

1943   D+ $1500
Cardboard   25" x 35"

#0072

1940   D+ $900

17" x 25"

#0073

1940   D $600

Easel Back   18" x 26"

#0074

1943   D $600

28" x 35"

#0075

1940   C+ $350

18" x 27"

#0076

1950   D $600

Self-Framed   27" x 21"

#0077

1950   D $600

Self-Framed   27" x 21"

#0078

1950   D $600

Self-Framed   27" x 21"

#0079

1950   C+ $500

Self-Framed   26" x 21"

#0080

1951   C+ $225

Self-Framed   19" x 21"

#0081

1906   D- $450

Back Bar   14" x 6"

#0082

1920   E $1000

11" x 5"

#0083

1933   E $900

16" x 10"

#0084

1936   D $400

8" x 16"

#0085

1936   D $400

8" x 16"

#0086

1936   D $400

8" x 16"

#0087

1936   D $400

8" x 16"

#0088

1940   C+ $400

George Petty   21" x 11"

#0090

1943   C+ $250

22" x 7"

#0089

1940   C+ $400

21" x 11"

#0091

1939   D $500

30" x 13"

#0093

1940   D+ $400

18" x 23"

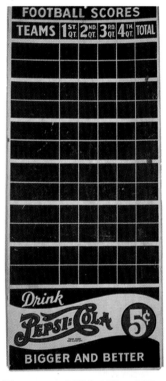

Reverse of #91 13" x 30"   **Reverse of #92 13" x 30"**

#0094

1940   D $350

11" x 6"

#0095

1940   C+ $350

12" x 6"

#0092

1940   C+ $450

30" x 13"

#0096

1940   C+ $350

12" x 6"

#0097

1943   D $100

11" x 14"

#0098

1945   D $150

11" x 14"

#0099

1945   D $150

11" x 14"

#0100

1945   D $125

11" x 14"

#0101

1950   D $150

14" x 11"

#0102

1951   C- $35

11" x 14"

#0103

1951   C+ $75

11" x 14"

#0104

1951   C+ $85

19" x 21"

#0105

1951   C+ $85

19" x 21"

#0106

1951   C $85

19" x 21"

#0107

1951   C $85

19" x 21"

#0108

1951   C+ $85

19" x 21"

#0109

1956   C $50

11" x 14"

#0110

1956   C $50

11" x 14"

#0111

1954   C+ $85

20" x 20"

#0112

1954   C $45

11" x 14"

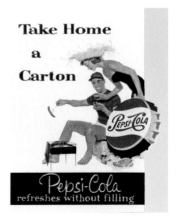

#0113

1954   C $50

11" x 14"

#0114

1954   C $50

16" x 20"

CARDBOARD INSERTS

Inserts are cardboard signs that were produced to fit into frames. At first, wood frames were used, followed by metal frames. Previous to this, these types of signs were called tackers, because they were actually tacked to the walls. It was believed that the signs placed in frames would receive better recognition. The frames also helped preserve and protect the cardboard. These inserts were produced in two sizes. The large inserts were 37" x 25". The small inserts were 28" x 11". Any sign with different measurements was most likely designed as a tacker, car, bus, or trolley sign, rather than an insert sign.

#0115

1958   B $25

Frame Only 37" x 25"

#0116

1945   D+ $650

37" x 25" Wood Frame

#0117

1945   D+ $850

37" x 25"

#0118

1945   D+ $850

Easel Back 37" x 25"

#0119

1949   D $850

37" x 25" Metal Frame

#0120

1949   D $850

37" x 25" Wood Frame

#0121

1950   C+ $500

27" x 21" Metal Frame

#0122

1950   C+ $500

37" x 25"

#0123

1951   C+ $300

37" x 25"

#0124

1951   C+ $300

37" x 25"

#0125

1951   D- $500

37" x 25"

#0126

1954   C $125

37" x 25"

#0127

1954   C $175

Double-Sided 37" x 25"

#0128

1954   C $175

Double-Sided 37" x 25"

#0129

1954   C $175

Double-Sided 37" x 25"

#0130

1954   C $175

Double-Sided 37" x 25"

#0131

1954   C $175

Double-Sided 37" x 25"

#0132

1954   D+ $125

18" x 23"

#0133

1954   C $175

Double-Sided 37" x 25"

#0134

1954   C $175

Double-Sided 37" x 25"

#0135

1954   C $175

Double-Sided 37" x 25"

#0136

1954   C $175

Double-Sided 37" x 25"

#0137

1958   C $125

37" x 25"

#0138

1958   C $125

37" x 25"

#0139

1961   B $50

37" x 25"

#0140

1964   B $45

37" x 25"

#0141

1964   B $45

25" x 37"

#0142

1963   B $45

25" x 37"

#0143

1970   C+ $100

22" x 28"

#0144

1940   D $500

28" x 11"

#0145

1940   D $500

28" x 11"

#0146

1940   D $500

28" x 11"

#0147

1940   D $500

28" x 11"

#0148

1943   D $500

28" x 11"

#0149

1943   D $500

28" x 11"

#0150

1943   D $500

28" x 11"

#0151

1943   D $500

28" x 11"

#0152

1943   D $500

28" x 11"

#0153

1943   D- $450

28" x 11"

#0154

1943   D $500

28" x 11"

#0155

1943   D $500

28" x 11"

#0156

1943   D $500

28" x 11"

#0157

1943   D $500

28" x 11"

#0158

1943   D $500

28" x 11"

#0159

1945   D $500

28" x 11"

#0160

1945   D- $450

28" x 11"

#0161

1945   D- $500

28" x 11"

#0162

1945   D $500

28" x 11"

#0163

1947   D $450

28" x 11"

#0164

1947   D $500

28" x 11" Wood Frame

#0165

1947   D $500

28" x 11" Wood Frame

#0166

1949   D $500

28" x 11"

#0167

1949   D $500

28" x 11"

#0168

1949   D $500

28" x 11"

#0169

1949   D $500

28" x 11"

#0170

1949   D $500

28" x 11"

#0171

1949   D- $450

28" x 11"

#0172

1950   C+ $350

28" x 11"

#0173

1950   D $350

28" x 11"

#0174

1951   C+ $150

28" x 11"

#0175

1954   B $75

28" x 11"

#0176

1954   B $75

28" x 11"

#0177

1954   B $75

28" x 11"

#0178

1954   B $75

28" x 11"

#0179

1954   B $75

28" x 11"

#0180

1954   B $75

28" x 11"

#0181

1954   B $75

28" x 11"

#0182

1958   B $75

28" x 11" Metal Frame

#0183

1958   B $75

28" x 11" Metal Frame

#0184

1960   C $75

28" x 11"

#0185

1961   B $30

28" x 11"

#0186

1964   B $30

28" x 11"

#0187

1963   B $30

28" x 11"

#0188

1963   B $30

28" x 11" Metal Frame

#0189

1964   B $30

28" x 11"

#0190

1964   B $30

28" x 11"

#0191

1964   B $30

28" x 11"

#0192

1967   B $30

28" x 11"

#0193

1967   B $30

28" x 11"

#0194

1967   B $30

28" x 11"

#0195

1971   B $30

28" x 11"

#0196

1971   B $30

28" x 11"

#0197

1971   B $30

28" x 11"

#0198

1976   B $20

28" x 11"

#0199

1976   B $20

28" x 11"

NEON CLOCKS

Clocks are among the oldest and most popular of advertising signage. Most retail stores were eager to hang a clock in their establishment. Clocks have been used as a way to advertise consumer products for decades, and the reason is obvious: Every time you look up to see the time, you see the advertisement. There is no accurate record of when Pepsi-Cola began advertising on clocks. It wasn't until 1940 that this form of advertising became a regular practice for the Pepsi-Cola Company. Within the clock category, there are two that have become very popular among collectors of advertising—neon and double glass clocks.

#0200

1939   E $3800

#0201

1939   D $3200

Neon 18" x 18"

#0202

1939   D $3500

Neon 18" x 18"

#0203

1945   D $1500

Neon 18" x 18"

#0204

1940   E $700

33" x 16"

#0205

1940   E $450

Wood Frame 15" x 15"

#0206

1940   C $250

15" x 15"

#0207

1945   C $400

Glass 15" Dia.

#0208

1945   D $350

15" x 15"

#0209

1947   C+ $300

14" x 14"

#0210

1947   D- $450

Hood Light 14" x 17"

#0211

1951   C+ $275

Light-Up 14" x 20"

#0212

1951   D $450

17" Dia.

#0213

1951   E $750

Light-Up 25" x 17"

#0214

1951   D- $600

20" Dia.

#0215

1951   C+ $900

Neon 35" Dia.

#0216

1960   C+ $900

Neon 35" Dia.

#0217

1951   D $250.

Plastic Light-Up 11" Dia.

#0218

1951   D- $750.

Glass 15" Dia.

#0219
1951   E $1500
Double Glass 15" Dia.

#0220
1954   D+ $500
Plastic 15" Dia.

#0221
1954   C+ $350
20" Dia.

#0222
1954   D+ $500
Plastic 15" Dia.

#0223
1954   C $225
18" Dia.

#0224
1954   C $250
Metal 15" x 15"

#0225
1959   D- $1400
Pam Clock 15" Dia.

#0226
1959   C+ $200
Light-Up 16" x 16"

#0227
1960   D- $1400
Double Glass 15" Dia.

#0228
1954   C $75
Light-Up 9" x 12"

#0229
1960   C+ $225
Glass 15" Dia.

#0230
1960   C+ $85
Light-Up 16" x 12"

#0231
1961   D- $1400
Double Glass 15" Dia.

#0232
1961   C+ $250
Plastic 16" x 16"

#0233
1964   D $1200
Double Glass 15" Dia.

#0234
1964   D+ $300
Light-Up 18" Dia.

#0235
1964   B+ $75
16" x 16"

#0236
1964   B+ $75
Light-Up 16" x 16"

#0237

1964   C $65

Light-Up 9" x 12"

#0238

1964   C+ $225

18" Dia.

#0239

1964   B+ $225

Light-Up 16" x 16"

#0240

1965   C $65

15" x 15"

#0241

1965   B+ $85

16" x 16"

#0242

1969   A $25

Plastic 16" x 15"

#0243

1973   C+ $200

Light- Up 16" x 16"

#0244

1973   C $50

Counter Clock 13" x 8"

#0245

1973   A $20

Light-Up 10" x 15"

CORBUF

Corbuf is single-face, corrugated cardboard. It is used at special events and to decorate displays. It is produced in 250' long rolls with varying heights. Each design is repeated every so many feet. To have a complete corrugated sign, you would need to have the entire design on one sheet. (See #0246).

#0246

1945   D $200

12" x 72"

#0247

1951   C+ $50

13" x 60"

#0248

1951   D- $75

30" x 60"

#0249

1954   C+ $25

30" x 48"

#0250

1954   C+ $25

30" x 48"

#0251

1965   C $20

30" x 48"

#0252

1965   C+ $30

18" x 36"

#0253

1965   C $20

24" x 36"

#0254

1973   B $10

24" x 36"

DECALS

Decals are among the most colorful of Pepsi signs. You will find decals in two forms—used and unused. The used are generally placed on glass to enable good viewing. This does not detract from the value. The unused will still be attached to the original backing. Occasionally, the image is face down on the backing material, making viewing impossible until the decal is transferred onto glass. Be careful with the water-transfer decals that are unused. Removing them from the backing is sometimes difficult and they can be damaged. You need to consider this when you are trying to determine how much to pay for an untransferred decal.

#0255

1936   D $350

7" x 4"

#0256

1936   D $350

7" x 4"

#0257

1937   D+ $500

Double-Sided 10"

#0258

1943   D+ $400

10" Dia.

#0259

1945   D $500

9" x 8"

#0260

1945   D $500

13" x 10"

#0261

1948   D $600

19" x 15"

#0262

1950   E $225

5" Tall

#0263

1950   E $225

5" Tall

#0264

1950   E $225

5" Tall

The five gorgeous girls
were issued as decals and as
cardboard signs. Either way,
they are extremely hard to
find. The decals were on one
sheet, perforated for easy
removal. These are found as
single decals, or more rarely
as a complete set.

#0265

1950   E $225

5" Tall

#0266

1950   E $225

5" Tall

#0267

1951   D+ $300

10" x 12"

#0268

1951   D $75

12" Dia.

#0269

1951   C+ $45

4" Dia.

#0270

1951   D $50
10" x 12"

#0271

1951   C+ $75
10" x 5"

#0272

1954   C+ $150
16" x 9"

#0273

1954   C+ $65
9" x 7"

#0274

1960   C+ $50
9" x 7"

#0275

1965   C+ $35
8" x 5"

#0276

1965   C+ $35
10" x 8"

#0277

1965   B $15
5" x 5"

#0278

1967   C $65
12" x 11"

This set of cardboard signs is known as a "festoon" (a decorative chain or strip hanging between two points). This is one of the rarest Pepsi signs known to exist. The sign consists of five, three-dimensional cardboard pieces linked together by a red and white cord. It is most likely that you will find individual pieces of the festoon, rather than the complete festoon. If you do, it is recommended that you buy the pieces, because even the individual pieces are rare.

#0279

1943   E+ $3500

96" x 48"

#0280

1954   C+ $225

Corrugated 96" x 32"

#0281

1954 D- $225

Corrugated 96" x 32"

#0282

1954 D $200

84" x 16" Fountain Valance

#0283

1954 C+ $50

5 Pieces Linked by Wire

#0284 and #0285 are both battery-operated, rotating displays.

#0284

1988 A $25

15" x 10"

#0285

1983 B+ $75

54" Tall

BOTTLE DISPLAYS

Bottle displays were used in what was called the cold bottle market. Normally, these were mom and pop stores, where people stopped in to get a cold drink. There are primarily two styles of bottle displays. One is where the bottle slips into the display, the other is where the display slides onto the neck of the bottle. Both styles are equally popular among collectors, which is reflected in their value. These signs are a great way to display old Pepsi bottles.

#0286

1936   E $550

13" Tall

#0287

1936   E $550

13" Tall

#0288

1928   E $950

13" Tall

#0289

1939   D $350

Foil Coated   14" Tall

#0290

1939   D- $350

Foil Coated   14" Tall

#0291

1940   D- $650

12" x 14"

#0292

1940   D $500

13" Tall

#0293

1940   D- $275

6" Tall

#0294

1940   D $125

6" x 8"

#0295

1939   D- $350

Foil Coated   14" Tall

#0296

1945   D+ $500

Foil Coated   14" Tall

#0297

1954   D+ $200

Light-Up 18" Tall

#0298

1957   D $450

16" x 20"

#0299

1957   D+ $500

16" x 68"

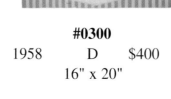

#0300

1958   D $400

16" x 20"

#0301

1983   C+ $50

14" Tall

RACKS AND RACK SIGNS

Metal racks were given to dealers as a way to increase orders and to get more display space. The popularity of these type of racks disappeared with the returnable bottles. It is very common to find rack signs only. Very often, the sign was removed from the rack and the rack was discarded. These display racks are very popular with collectors for displaying Pepsi collections.

These racks could be added together to build as large a display as necessary.

#0302

1940   D $400
36" x 35"

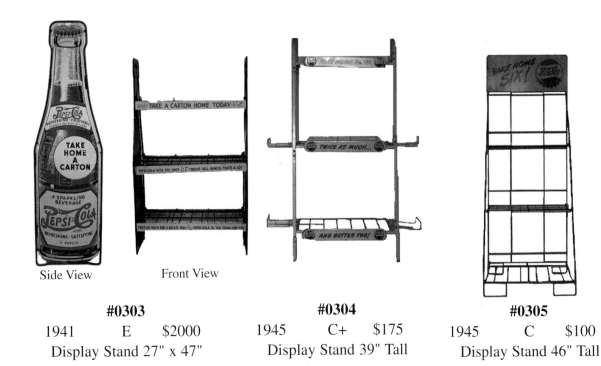

Side View   Front View

#0303

1941   E $2000
Display Stand 27" x 47"

#0304

1945   C+ $175
Display Stand 39" Tall

#0305

1945   C $100
Display Stand 46" Tall

#0306

1951   C- $75

18" x 40" x 12"

#0307

1960   C- $80

Display Stand 60" Tall

#0308

1934   C+ $125

Double-Sided 8" x 8"

#0309

1940   C $200

Double-Sided 16" x 6"

#0310

1940   C $200

Rack Sign 16" x 4"

#0311

1951   B+ $50

Rack Sign 18" x 5"

#0312

1945   C+ $300

22" x 14"

#0313

1951   C+ $100

Masonite 19" x 14"

#0314

1954   B $45

23" x 18"

#0315

1950   B $25

Metal 6" x 6"

#0316

1951   B $45

Double Sided 23" x 18"

#0317

1951   B+ $30

18" x 5"

#0318

1960   B+ $30

18" x 5"

#0319

1963   B+ $20

14" x 5"

#0320

1954   C $45

Metal 26" x 15"

#0321

1960   B $35

16" x 14"

#0322

1965   B $25

24" x 16"

#0323

1940   E $350

Door Pull 3" x 12"

#0324

1940   D $300

Door Pull 12" Tall

#0325

1940   D $300

Door Pull 4" x 12"

#0326

1940   D+ $300

Door Push 3" x 12"

#0327

1940   D+ $300

Door Push 3" x 10"

#0328

1940   D $300

Door Push 3" x 10"

#0329

1940   C+ $200

Door Push 3" x 10"

#0330   1940   E- $300

Door Push 26"

#0331   1940   E- $350

Porcelain 35"

#0332   1960   C $75

Adjustable

#0333   1951   C+ $75

Push Bar 30" x 8"

#0334   1965   C+ $100

Porcelain 32" x 3"

#0335   1973   B $35

Push Bar 30" x 5"

#0336

1954   D $65

Flower Display 10" x 8"

#0337

1954   C $35

Foil Easel Back 5" x 8"

#0338

1960   A $15

12" x 5"

#0339

1960   C $35

11" x 5"

#0340

1965   C $20

6" x 4"

#0341

1965   C $25

14" x 6"

#0342

1967   C $75

13" x 12"

#0343

1958   C+ $85

7" x 13"

#0344

1965   C $45

15" x 13"

FLANGE SIGNS

Flange signs are normally double-sided. They were used in key locations, where they could be viewed from both sides. Flange signs were used indoors and outdoors. For most collectors, flange signs are highly desirable, and demand premium prices.

#0345

1940   D+ $800

Metal 17" x 16"

#0346

1940   D+ $800

Metal 17" x 16"

#0347

1940   C+ $550

Metal 15" x 10"

#0348

1940   D+ $500

Metal 15" x 10"

#0349

1943   D+ $800

Metal 17" x 14"

#0350

1945   C+ $450

Masonite 13" x 12"

#0351

1945   D- $750

17" x 15"

#0352

1945   E $1000

17" x 14"

#0353

1951   D- $450

Masonite 44" x 16"

#0354

1951   C+ $450

Metal 15" x 14"

#0355

1951   C+ $450

Metal 15" x 14"

#0356

1963   C+ $350

Metal 18" x 15"

GLASS SIGNS

Glass signs are made by reverse printing on glass. This process creates a beautiful and attractive product. This is especially true when the printing is backed with the silver that produces mirrors. Due to the fragile nature of glass signs, these are the rarest and most difficult of Pepsi signs to find. Most often these were used at fountain locations or back bar displays.

#0357
1937   E $3500
Reverse Foil 12" x 10"

#0358
1940   D+ $750
Printed Reverse 10" x 5"

#0359
1943   D $300
Printed Reverse 19" x 9"

#0360
1940   D $300
Printed Reverse 11" x 5"

#0361
1943   D $400
Printed Reverse 10" x 5"

#0362
1963   C $50
Easel Plaque 8" x 11"

#0363
1964   C+ $100
Reverse Glass 14" x 14"

ADVERTISING MIRRORS

The key to a good advertising sign is to attract the attention of potential customers. Over the years, mirrors have done this as well as any other form of indoor signage. Pepsi advertising mirrors have become some of the most attractive signage offered by the company, thus, a popular choice for advertising at point of sale locations.

Mirrors are very popular to the collector because of their beauty and rarity. The rarity of Pepsi mirrors exists primarily for two reasons. The primary reason is the fragile nature of the glass. Secondly, the silver used to make mirrors tends to deteriorate over time, rendering the mirrors useless.

For all these reasons, Pepsi advertising mirrors make great collectibles.

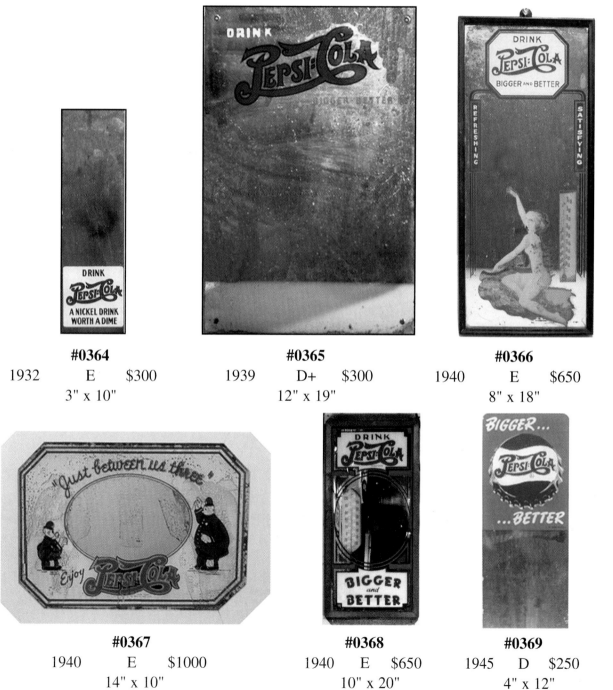

	#0364		
1932	E	$300	
	3" x 10"		

	#0365		
1939	D+	$300	
	12" x 19"		

	#0366		
1940	E	$650	
	8" x 18"		

	#0367		
1940	E	$1000	
	14" x 10"		

	#0368		
1940	E	$650	
	10" x 20"		

	#0369		
1945	D	$250	
	4" x 12"		

#0372
1950   D+ $100
10" x 8"

#0370
1945   D $250
6" x 13"

#0371
1950   D+ $150
6" x 8"

#0373
1951   D+ $125
6" x 17"

#0375
1954   C $65
6" x 10"

#0374
1954   C $85
6" x 14"

#0376
1981   A $15
14" x 20"

ILLUMINATED SIGNS

Illuminated signs, also known as light-up signs, are among the most expensive of Pepsi-Cola collectibles. This is due, in part, to the popularity of light-up signs among collectors. In this category, there is a myriad of different types. There are neon, rotating, glass, plastic, and double-sided signs. They all serve different purposes. Among these types, neon and rotating signs are the most sought-after.

#0377

1940   E $3000

Glass 14" x 7"

#0378

1940   E $800

Neon 14" x 5"

#0379

1940   D $600

25" x 7"

#0380

1940   D+ $800

16" x 13"

#0381

1940   D+ $700

13" x 9"

#0382

1940   E $1500

Revolving Light 16" x 10"

#0383

1940   D+ $800

19" x 8"

#0384

1940   E $750

Neon 22" x 8"

#0385

1941   E $1800

Neon

#0386

1945   D+ $800

26" x 7"

#0387

1951   D $350

Plastic 8" x 8"

#0388

1951   D- $500

Reverse Glass 12" x 12"

#0389

1951   D $750

12" x 12"

#0390

1951   E- $2500

21" x 10"

#0391

1951   D $400

Plastic 15"

#0392

1951   C+ $85

Double-Sided 17" x 13"

#0393

1953   D $600

Plastic 21" x 18"

#0394

1956   C $100

18" x 14"

#0395

1954   D $150

Plastic 26" x 8"

#0396

1954   D $450

Double Sided 42" x 10"

#0397

1954   C+ $90

Plastic 5" x 11"

#0398

1954   C $250

Plastic 48" x 12"

#0399

1954   C+ $250

Plastic 60" x 12"

#0400

1954   C $250

Plastic 48" x 10"

#0401

1954   C+ $275

Plastic 19" x 9"

#0402

1954   C+ $275

Plastic 19" x 9"

#0403

1954   C+ $150

Plastic 23" x 9"

#0404

1954   D $1500

Double-Sided 24" x 18"

#0405

1954   D $1500

Double-Sided 14" x 6"

#0406

1954   C+ $275

Plastic 26" x 12"

#0407

1954   C+ $275

Plastic 26" x 12"

#0408

1954   D $300

Plastic 24" x 8"

#0409

1954   C+ $300

Plastic 10" x 18"

#0410

1954   D $400

Plastic 15" Dia.

70

#0411

1954   D $350

12" x 12" Rotates

#0412

1954   D $350

10" x 13" Rotates

#0413

1954   D $350

10" x 13" Rotates

#0414

1958   C+ $125

Plastic 9" x 12"

#0415

1956   C $150

Plastic 12" x 9"

#0416

1960   B $65

Plastic 9" x 12"

#0417

1954   C+ $450

21" x 7"

#0418

1954   C+ $450

21" x 7"

#0419

1954   C+ $450

21" x 7"

#0420

1954   C+ $450

21" x 7"

The base of these signs was standard, enabling a number of different foil-laminated pieces to be connected based on the bottler's need.

#0421

1954   C+ $450

21" x 7"

#0422

1960   C $300

26" x 26"

#0423

1963   D+ $800

Rotating 16" Tall

#0424

1969   D+ $225

7" x 8"

#0425

1965   C+ $150

Plastic 24" x 16"

#0426

1964   C+ $475

Light/Clock 26" x 26"

#0427

1975   C+ $500

Neon

#0428

1975   C+ $300

52" x 12"

#0429

1975   C $75

20" x 26"

MENU BOARDS

Menu boards are among the few advertising signs that actually serve a function. They were placed in restaurants, grocery stores, and gas stations, where besides advertising Pepsi-Cola, they could list prices or specials. Because of this, they were very popular among Pepsi vendors. To meet this demand, Pepsi produced various styles. Some are strictly menu boards, while others are slate boards that can be used to write on. Menu boards are available in wood, metal, and glass. They range in price from inexpensive to very expensive.

#0430

1939   D $400
20" x 30"

#0431

1940   D $400
20" x 30"

#0432

1940   D $400
20" x 30"

#0433

1940   D+ $400
20" x 30"

#0434

1940   D+ $450
20" x 30"

#0435

1945   C+ $250
15" x 23"

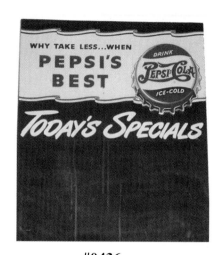

#0436

1945   D+ $450

19" x 23"

#0437

1945   C+ $250

19" x 28"

#0438

1950   D- $300

20" x 30"

#0439

1951   C $175

20" x 30"

#0440

1954   C $150

20" x 30"

#0441

1954   D $150

Cardboard 20" x 30"

#0442

1954   B $125

20" x 30"

#0443

1960   B $95

20" x 30"

#0444

1960   B $95

20" x 30"

#0445

1963   A $75

20" x 30"

#0446

1965   A $65

20" x 30"

#0447

1965   A $65

20" x 30"

#0448

1965   B+ $50

20" x 30"

#0449

1973   A $40

20" x 30"

#0450

1991   A $20

20" x 30"

#0451

1943   D $500

Wood 25" x 20"

#0452

1943   D+ $475

Wood 12" x 24"

#0453

1945   D $350

Cardboard 13" x 21"

#0454

1945   E $750

Cardboard 10" x 20"

#0455

1951   D+ $300

Wood 9" x 23"

#0456

1954   C+ $350

Glass 36" x 20"

#0457

1954   D $250

Glass 9" x 18"

#0458

1954   C+ $175

Light-Up 30" x 24"

#0459

1954   C+ $175

Light-Up 30" x 24"

#0460

1965   B $25

32" x 12"

#0461

1970   B $10

28" x 10"

#0462

1905   E+ $1800

10" x 8"

#0463

1906   E $800

9" x 5"

#0464

1910   D+ $300

12" x 3"

#0465

1910   D $450

10" x 4"

#0466

1910   D $500

28" x 10"

#0467

1910   D $700

28" x 6"

#0468

1935   E $400

20" x 3"

#0469

1936   D $400

17" x 6"

#0470

1940   C+ $350

14" x 5"

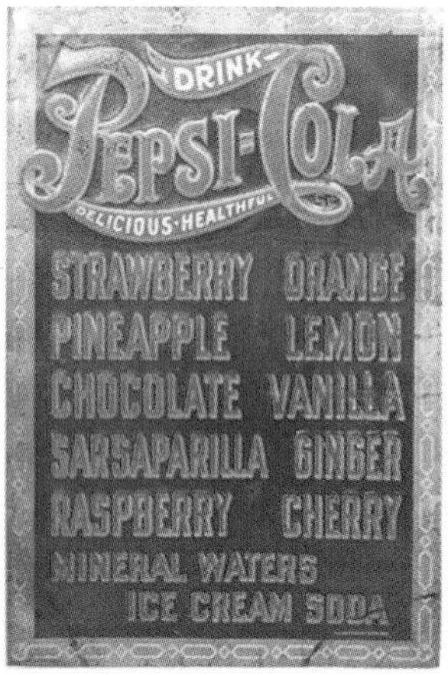

#0471
1915 E $800
12" x 23"

#0472
1939 E $800
20" x 20"

#0473
1940 C+ $250
20" x 13"

#0474
1940 C+ $350
13" x 9"

#0475
1950 D+ $425
Kick Plate 11" Tall

#0476
1950 D+ $425
Kick Plate 11" Tall

#0477
1950 D+ $425
Kick Plate 11" Tall

#0478
1951 C+ $175
12" x 15"

#0479

1910   D+ $800

28" x 20"

#0480

1909   D+ $500

16" x 8"

#0481

1909   E $1000

27" x 12"

#0482

1909   D $500

18" x 9"

#0483

1928   D+ $700

27" x 13"

#0484

1939   D $350

23" x 12"

#0485

1939   D+ $750

20" x 14"

#0486

1940   D+ $600

46" x 29"

#0487

1940   D+ $450

47" x 29"

#0488

1939   D- $550

28" x 20"

#0489

1940   D- $500

40" x 22"

#0490

1940   D- $600

40" x 22"

#0491

1945   C+ $250

28" x 20"

#0492

1945   D $350
19" x 27"

#0493

1953   D+ $275
23" x 23"

#0494

1951   C+ $150
36" x 36"

#0495

1951   C+ $150
34" x 20"

#0496

1936   E $500
13" x 29"

#0497

1936   D+ $900
Die-Cut 29" Tall

#0498

1940   D+ $900
Die-Cut 29" Tall

#0499

1942   D+ $900
Die-Cut 29" Tall

#0500

1945   D+ $900
Die-Cut 29" Tall

#0501

1936   D $900

Die-Cut 45" Tall

#0502

1941   D $800

Die-Cut 45" Tall

#0503

1945   D+ $700

Die-Cut 45" Tall

#0504

1929   E $2000

13" x 39"

#0505

1936   D+ $750

11" x 49"

#0506

1936   D+ $750

16" x 49"

#0507

1941   D $600

26" x 60"

#0508

1941   D $750

16" x 49"

#0509

1950   D+ $600

14" x 52"

#0510

1951   C+ $350

18" x 48"

#0511

1951   C+ $350

18" x 52"

#0512

1954   C $200

18" x 48"

#0513

1958   C $225

18" x 48"

#0514

1958   C $225

18" x 48"

#0515

1965   C $200

18" x 48"

#0516

1940   D $800

96" x 48"

#0517

1939   C+ $400

56" x 33"

#0518

1940   C+ $400

56" x 33"

#0519

1949   D- $400

43" x 51"

#0520

1951   D- $350

Self Framed 72" x 36"

#0521

1951   C $250

50" x 36"

#0522

1954   C+ $200

72" x 36"

#0523
1951   C $250
Die Cut 41" x 51"

#0524
1960   C $175
41" x 51"

#0525
1965   C+ $225
40" x 36"

#0526
1965   C+ $225
40" x 36"

#0527
1969   B $75
38" x 60"

#0528
1991   A $30
22" x 30"

#0529

1910   E $5000

39" x 14"

#0530

1939   D+ $1200

30" x 20"

#0531

1929   D+ $500

28" x 20"

#0532

1936   D+ $1000

36" x 24"

#0533

1939   D+ $650

36" x 14"

#0534

1940   D+ $600

36" x 14"

#0535

1945   C+ $300

26" x 10"

#0536

1945   C+ $300

29" x 11"

#0537

1948   C+ $600

36" x 14"

#0538

1951   C+ $350

36" x 14"

#0539

1951   C+ $125

28" x 12"

#0540

1951   C+ $100

28" x 12"

#0541

1951   C+ $95

28" x 12"

#0542

1960   C+ $65

31" x 12"

#0543

1960   C+ $65

31" x 12"

#0544

1963   B+ $50

31" x 12"

#0545

1965   B+ $50

31" x 12"

#0546

1973   B+ $40

31" x 12"

#0547

1950   D- $300

27" x 27"

#0548

1950   D+ $300

30" x 27"

#0549

1951   C $250

25" x 26"

#0550

1951   C $225

25" x 26"

#0551

1960   C+ $200

27" x 30"

#0552

1960   E $200

27" x 30"

#0553

1960   C+ $200

27" x 30"

#0554

1964   C $65

27" x 30"

#0555

1965   B $45

27" x 30"

#0556

1951   C $200

18" Dia.

#0557

1951   C $200

18" Dia.

#0558

1963   C $100

40" x 16"

#0559

1958   D $800

12 Feet Tall

#0560

1954   D+ $1500

30" x 64"

Reverse of #0560

CURB STAND SIGNS

Curb stand signs were designed to fit in a frame that was set out on a sidewalk. Each frame normally held two signs back to back. This enabled a passerby to see the Pepsi sign from both directions. Additionally, curb stand signs were made bearing different phrases. Over the years, most of these frames were discarded, while many of the signs survived. To find these signs in a frame is very rare. You can expect to pay top dollar for a complete set.

Besides the curb service sign, Pepsi also produced similar signs with the following text:

Curb Service
Sold Here
Cigars - Cigarettes
Candy - Ice Cream
Sandwiches - Cold Drinks
Hot Dogs - Hamburgers
Groceries - Meats
Groceries - Vegetables
Groceries
Blank - Dealer Privilege
Curb Service
Curb Service (without 5 cents)
Sold Here
Blank Dealer Privilege
Slate
Standard For Curb Sign

On all curb stand signs, the basic design remained the same. The changes occurred in the top and bottom lines. Two signs were needed for each standard and inserted back to back.

#0561
1940   D $750
Display/Frame 20" x 28"

#0562
1940   D $500
Display/Frame 20" x 28"

Advertising bulletins like this were used to alert Pepsi-Cola bottlers to the availability of the latest advertising materials. These bulletins informed bottlers of everything from size to price. In many cases, they would suggest the best usage of the advertising item. The sign featured in this bulletin sold for 39 cents in 1941.

#0563

1940   D+ $600

49" x 16"

#0564

1929 $1000

39" x 16"

#0565

1939   D+ $700

38" x 12"

#0566

1951   C+ $225

49" x 16"

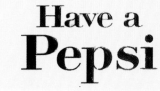

#0567

1960   C+ $200

49" x 16"

#0568

1954   C+ $200

49" x 16"

#0569

1939   E $600

11" x 3"

#0570

1940   D+ $350

6" x 6"

#0571

1943   D+ $250

8" x 6"

#0572

1939   E $400

10" x 4"

#0573

1940   D $650

Cardboard 10" x 6"

#0574

1940   D+ $575

Cash Register Top 12" x 5"

#0575

1940   D $400

Hanger 15" x 15"

#0576

1940   D $600

Double Sided 15" x 15"

#0577

1950   D+ $500

3-D Masonite 20" x 12"

#0578

1963   C+ $125

Mileage Chart 30" Tall

#0579

1939   E $1200

Bag Holder 23" x 13"

#0580

1945   D- $500

Bag Holder 36" x 16"

#0581

1940   C+ $350

String Holder 14" x 16"

#0582

1940   E $800

String Holder 14" x 16"

#0583

1945   D $250

Wood 60" x 30"

FAN PULLS

Fan pulls were fastened to the end of the fan chain to make the chain easy to grab. These pulls were also used on light cords and for decorations.

#0584

| 1940 | E | $500 |

Fan Pull 4" x 7"

#0585

| 1945 | C+ | $45 |

Cardboard Fan Pull 4"

#0586

| 1945 | C- | $55 |

Plastic Fan Pull 3"

#0587

| 1945 | D | $75 |

Calendar Holder 3"

#0588

| 1951 | C- | $45 |

Plastic Fan Pull 3"

#0589

| 1951 | D | $55 |

Calendar Holder 3"

#0590

| 1951 | C+ | $20 |

10" Tall

#0591

| 1951 | B | $10 |

Cardboard 4"

#0592

1943   D $300

Heavy Paper 60" x 30"

#0593

1950   D+ $350

Heavy Paper 65" x 20"

#0594

1950   C+ $225

Heavy Paper 20" x 28"

#0595

1969   D $100

27" x 35"

#0596   1951   C+ $85

Heavy Paper 65" x 20"

#0597   1951   C+ $75

63" x 13"

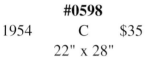

#0598

1954   C $35

22" x 28"

#0599

1956   C $20

14" x 20"

#0600

1956   C $20

20" x 14"

#0601

1954   C $20

14" x 20"

#0602

1954   C $20

14" x 20"

#0603

1954   C $25

14" x 20"

#0604

1951   C $25

8" x 18"

#0605

1951   C+ $25

22" x 7"

#0606

1937   E $200

18" x 6"

#0607

1948   C $35

20" x 9"

#0608

1947   C+ $50

28" x 11"

#0609

1951   A $20

20" x 9"

#0610

1949   C $40

20" x 9"

#0611

1951   C $30

22" x 7"

#0612

1951   C $30

20" x 8"

#0613

1954   B $20

22" x 7"

#0614

1954   C $35

20" x 8"

#0615

1956   B $20

20" x 8"

#0616

1954   B $10

22" x 7"

#0617

1954   B $20

22" x 7"

#0618

1954   C $35

20" x 8"

#0619

1959   C $35

22" x 7"

#0620

1975   C $10

20" x 8"

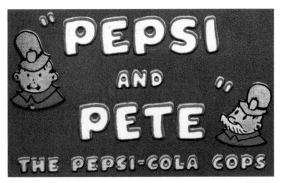

The success of the 12-ounce bottle for a nickel resulted in Pepsi-Cola becoming a major participant in consumer advertising. Almost overnight, the Pepsi-Cola Company had to develop a new and better advertising program. One of the most popular ideas was to use a cartoon character in the Sunday funnies. The first thought was to buy Popeye the Sailor Man, and have him drink Pepsi in place of spinach. Unfortunately for Pepsi, the cost of Popeye switching from spinach to Pepsi was more than the company could afford. Pepsi management decided that they would create their own cartoon characters.

Many ideas were bounced around, from animals to children, and finally Pepsi settled on two Keystone Cop-style characters. Walter Mack, the president of the Pepsi-Cola Company at that time, decided they should be named Pepsi and Pete. So, in the fall of 1939, Pepsi and Pete made their premier appearance in magazine and newspaper ads.

From 1939 until 1951, Pepsi and Pete were featured in the comic section of the Sunday newspapers around the country. Various artists were used to draw Pepsi and Pete, including one of the most famous during that period - Rube Goldberg. The popularity of Pepsi and Pete brought about greater usage of the Pepsi-Cola cops in magazine advertising, point of purchase materials, give-away novelties, and even an animated commercial shown at movie theaters during intermission.

Today Pepsi and Pete memorabilia is at the top of the "want list" for many Pepsi collectors. Currently, Pepsi and Pete memorabilia is commanding top dollar for anything bearing the likeness of these two loveable characters.

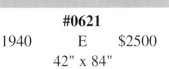

#0621			#0622			#0623		
1940	E	$2500	1940	E	$2500	1940	E	$2500
42" x 84"			42" x 84"			42" x 84"		

Pepsi & Pete Festoon - seven cardboard cut outs printed on two sides, and linked together by a string spanning 108". The cardboard pieces can be found individually priced between $200-$400. But be careful! Some have been reproduced!

#0624   1940   E $4000

#0625	**#0626**	**#0627**
1940 D- $1200	1940 D $1800	1940 E $1200
11" x 15"	22" x 15"	10" x 21"

#0628	**#0629**	**#0630**
1940 D $450	1940 D $450	1940 E $750
7" x 8"	7" x 8"	9" x 14"

#0631

1940   D+ $650

21" x 11"

#0632

1940   E $700

28" x 11"

#0633

1940   D+ $650

21" x 11"

#0634

1943   E $700

28" x 11"

#0635

1939   C+ $350

Embossed 21" x 14"

#0636 mounts on a stand, and is double-sided. Only a few of these are known to exist.

#0636

1940   E+ $3500

36" x 72"

PLAQUES

These advertising plaques are commonly referred to as celluloids. Celluloid is a trade name for a plastic-like substance, and it is one of the components used in producing these signs. A clear plastic coating is placed on top of a round, metal disk with a cardboard backing. These can either be hung from an attached cord or as a standing display using the easel on back.

#0637
1936   D $800
Easel Back 5" x 13"

#0638
1940   D $400
9" Dia.

#0639
1945   E $500
9" Dia.

#0640
1945   C+ $350
9" Dia.

#0641
1948   C+ $350
9" Dia.

#0642
1951   C+ $300
9" Dia.

#0643
1951   C+ $275
9" Dia.

#0644

1954   C+ $85

Easel Back 8" x 12"

#0645

1954   C+ $100

Easel Back 8" x 12"

#0646

1960   B+ $45

Easel Back 11" x 9"

#0647

1960   B+ $45

Easel Back 11" x 9"

#0648

1961   C $50

Easel Back 8" x 12"

#0649

1963   B $35

Easel Back 10" x 12"

#0650

1965   B $35

Easel Back 10" x 12"

#0651

1967   C $45

Easel Back 8" x 12"

#0652

1969   C $45

Easel Back 12" x 8"

#0653
1945   D+ $600
Easel Back 9" x 12"

#0654
1951   B+ $35
Conversion Plate 9" x 4"

#0655
1951   C+ $75
Fountain Sign 9" x 9"

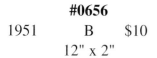

#0656
1951   B $10
12" x 2"

#0657
1953   D- $250
Machine Sign 30" x 13"

#0658
1953   D- $75
Machine Sign 30" x 13"

#0659
1954   C $100
Two-View Plaque 10" Dia.

Reverse View

#0660
1954   D $100
15" x 10"

#0661

1958   C+ $75

16" x 13"

#0662

1958   B+ $15

13" x 10"

#0663

1965   C $45

12" x 10"

#0664

1965   C $45

Plastic 9" x 11"

#0665

1965   C $45

11" x 9"

#0666

1965   C $35

10" x 11"

#0667

1965   C $45

Plastic 9" x 11"

#0668

1965   C $45

Plastic 9" x 11"

#0669

1965   C $45

10" x 12"

#0670

1965   B $20

12" x 10"

#0671

1965   B+ $20

14" x 10"

#0672

1965   C+ $25

12" x 10"

#0673

1965   C+ $65

13" x 8"

#0674

1965   B+ $15

18" x 20"

#0675

1965   B+ $15

18" x 20"

#0676

1965   D $100

10" x 18"

#0677

1967   D $100

14" x 14"

#0678

1967   D $100

12" x 5"

#0679

1969   A $10

18" x 20"

#0680

1969   B $10

19" x 18"

#0681

1969   B $10

19" x 18"

#0682

1973   A $5

10" x 8"

#0683

1973   B $15

16" x 19"

#0684

1973   A $5

12" x 12"

#0685

1973   B $25

44" x 10"

#0686

1973   A $5

10" x 8"

PORCELAIN SIGNS

These signs are probably the most durable and most expensive signs Pepsi ever produced. They were designed to be used in in extreme climates outdoors. For these reasons, smaller quantities of these signs were made. As a result, porcelain signs are rare and very valuable.

#0688

1940   E $350
20" x 8"

#0687

1934   E $1200
40" x 30"

#0690

1945   D $400
18" x 6"

#0689

1945   E $500
36" x 12"

#0692

1945   D+ $500
42" Dia.

#0691

1945   D $800
48" x 30"

#0693

1950   D+ $100
38" x 14"

#0695

1951   D $600

36" Dia.

#0694

1950   D+ $1000

18" x 48"

#0696

1951   D $600

36" Dia.

#0697

1960   D $400

40" x 40"

#0698

1969   C+ $350

Die Cut 18" x 42"

#699

1950   D $150

13" Tall

#700

1950   C+ $125

27" x 21"

#701

1951   C+ $100

28" x 11"

#703

1951   C+ $55

20" Tall

#702

1953   C $50

20" Tall

#704

1954   C+ $85

26" Tall

#705

1956   C $45

20" Tall

#706

1958   B+ $35

20" Tall

#707

1963   C+ $65

20" Tall

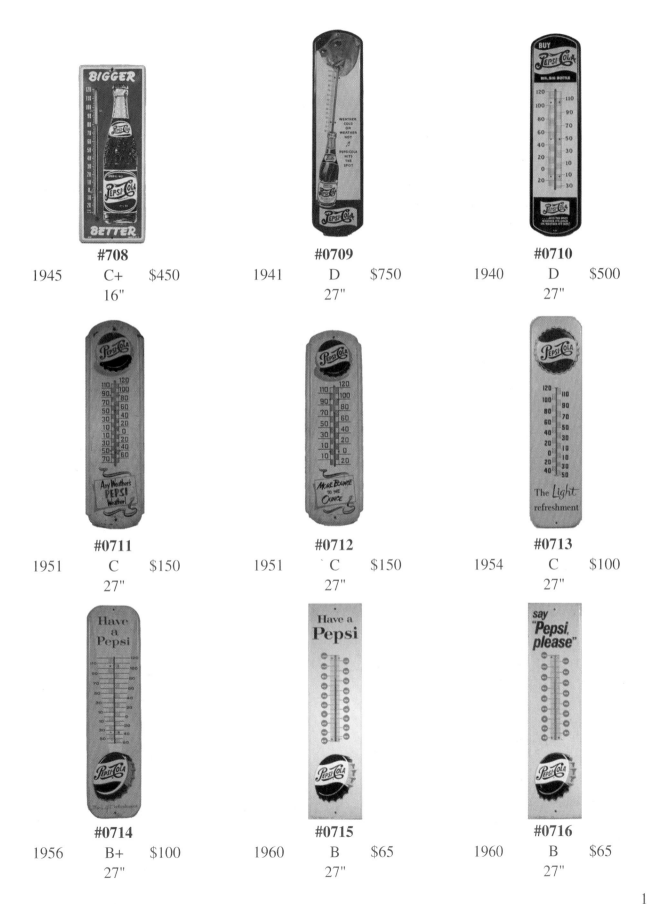

#708

1945   C+ $450
      16"

#0709

1941   D $750
      27"

#0710

1940   D $500
      27"

#0711

1951   C $150
      27"

#0712

1951   C $150
      27"

#0713

1954   C $100
      27"

#0714

1956   B+ $100
      27"

#0715

1960   B $65
      27"

#0716

1960   B $65
      27"

#0717

1964	B	$60
27"		

#0718

1965	B	$50
28"		

#0719

1991	A	$25
27"		

#0720

1945	D	$175
18"		

#0721

1951	D	$450
12" Dia.		

#0722

1965	D-	$75
18" Dia.		

#0723

1965	A	$15
9" x 9"		

#0724

1971	A	$10
10" x 10"		

#0725

1975	A	$45
18" Dia.		

It is no accident that Containers follows Signs in this book, because the two go hand in hand. Containers, like signs, play an integral part in the marketing of Pepsi-Cola. Bottles, cans, dispensers, and vending machines all serve a dual purpose as containers and signs. In fact, even though these items were designed by engineers, the graphics and color schemes were created by advertising people. After all, getting a consumer to reach for a bottle or six-pack of Pepsi-Cola is more about attractive packaging than the structural qualities of the container.

In addition to information and prices on containers, this section offers examples of the evolution of Pepsi packaging. You can follow the changes in style and sizes of bottles from the first bottle in 1905, through the non-returnable bottles introduced in the early 1960s. In 1939, Pepsi-Cola introduced their first 6-bottle carton. Over the next 50 plus years, there have been numerous changes in both size and style of Pepsi cartons. Twelve-packs are one the of the most popular forms of Pepsi packaging today. Twelve-packs were originally designed for bottles in 1947. The first Pepsi-Cola cans were cone-top shaped, so they could be filled by standard bottling equipment.

In many ways, containers and packaging mirrors the history of our time. During the great depression, value-packaging was essential. The World War II years presented opportunities for efficient and reusable containers. The post-war years saw image and style become the dominant characteristic of Pepsi containers. In 1958, the swirl bottle was introduced. With the 1960s, came the need for convenient packaging. Cans and non-returnable bottles led the way.

CONTAINERS

HISTORY OF PEPSI-COLA BOTTLES

It may be said that in the history of business, no other packaging has been important to a company as the bottle has been to the Pepsi-Cola Company. From the early days of Pepsi-Cola, when Coca-Cola controlled the fountain business, it was the bottle that made Pepsi-Cola an important soft drink company. In the desperate days of the great depression, it was the use of the 12-ounce bottle that gave Pepsi-Cola a new beginning, resulting in the company becoming one of the largest soft drink companies in the world. The bottle has played a major role in Pepsi-Cola's history. It is also an important part of Pepsi-Cola collecting. No matter what your passion or interest is in Pepsi-Collectibles, you probably own at least one Pepsi bottle, and in some cases, hundreds of Pepsi bottles. Bottles tell the story of Pepsi-Cola better than any other collectible. The style, shape, and color were the results of the conditions at the Pepsi-Cola Company when a particular bottle was used. From production to prototype bottles, they all make collecting Pepsi-Cola bottles so much fun.

THE 6-OUNCE BOTTLE ERA
1905-1933

From 1905 to 1933, the predominant size bottles sold by the Pepsi-Cola Company and affiliated Pepsi-Cola bottlers was 6 ounces. However, many bottlers used a variety of sizes, including 6-1/2, 7, and 9-ounce bottles, depending on what was popular in their bottling territory. The shape and color of these bottles was more the result of what local glass manufacturers produced, rather than a desire by the Pepsi-Cola Company for uniformity. During this time, bottlers generally had the name Pepsi-Cola embossed in the glass along with the name of the franchise. Each bottle was supposed to be decorated with a diamond-shaped paper label. Because of the labor involved, many times the labels were left off.

From 1923 to 1931, Pepsi-Cola headquarters was in Richmond, Virginia. During this time, there was an effort to use a standardized bottle. Because of a difficult financial situation, the standardized bottle was never completely implemented.

1905

1928

1929

THE 12-OUNCE BOTTLE ERA
1934-1964

From the inception of bottled soft drinks, the standard size was a 6-ounce bottle. This all changed in 1934, when Pepsi offered the first 12-ounce bottle for a nickel. The first 12-ounce Pepsi bottles were used beer bottles. These bottles came in green, amber, and clear colors. Each bottle was decorated with a paper label bearing the Pepsi-Cola trademark. Due to the fragility of the paper label, most of these bottles have perished. This makes the paper label beer bottles very collectible and highly valuable.

In 1940, Pepsi introduced their first standardized bottle. This new 12-ounce bottle had Pepsi-Cola blown into the neck with a paper label on the neck and body. During World War II, the equipment necessary to apply graphics directly the bottle was developed. Following the war, this technique was used throughout the Pepsi-Cola system. These bottles were referred to as ACL (Applied Color Label) bottles.

In 1951, Pepsi underwent an effort to modernize the company. This resulted in a major change in the Pepsi-Cola script logo. Besides being sleeker, the new logo now only had one hyphen between Pepsi and Cola. This new logo was used on standard Pepsi bottles from 1951 to 1957.

The year 1958 brought about a major change in the Pepsi bottle design. A new, modern-looking bottle was introduced. It was called the "swirl" bottle, because of the way the glass swirled around the bottle. The swirl bottle was used from 1958 through 1978. It was the last returnable bottle design ever used by the Pepsi-Cola Company.

In the 1960s, non-returnable bottles and cans began to replace the returnable bottle in popularity. Although the 12-ounce bottle was the predominant bottle used by the Pepsi-Cola Company during this period, other sizes were used in various markets throughout the United States. The sizes used were 6-1/2-, 8-, 10-, 16-, 26-, and 32-ounces.

1934   1936   1939   1940

1943

1945

1951

1958

THE NON-RETURNABLE BOTTLE ERA
1964 - Present

Non-returnable bottles, or no deposit bottles, had been test-marketed as far back as the late 1940s. However, it wasn't until 1964 that it was decided to make non-returnables an option for Pepsi-Cola bottlers. By 1964, automobiles had made America the most mobile society in history. With this new mobility came the need for more convenient soft drink containers. Non-returnables were the perfect solution. These smaller and lighter bottles could hold as much as the larger, heavier returnables, and with no-deposit, they could be disposed of anywhere. In the past thirty years, numerous styles and shapes of non-returnable bottles have been produced. But, they lack the beauty and historical importance of the returnable bottles. Non-returnable bottles have never been as dominant as their predecessors, the returnable bottles. This is due to the popularity of the disposable aluminum cans.

1965

PRICING

Non-returnable bottles have very limited monetary value as Pepsi collectibles. There are some exceptions. Early test market and prototype non-returnable bottles are considerably more valuable. You can expect to pay for between $1 and $5 for most non-returnables bottles.

408

WHERE MANUFACTURED   YEAR

Back of bottle

DES. PAT. 120,277

14 9 47

23 ◊ 118

Duraglas

951-G

MANUFACTURER

Bottom of bottle

This chart is for identification and dating of Pepsi bottles produced in the 1950s. The first two numbers on the back of the bottle designate the location and name of the bottle manufacturing facility. The third number corresponds with the year it was produced. In this case, the "8" is 1958. If the number does not appear on the back of the bottle, you can locate manufacturing and production dates from the codes on the bottom of the bottle.

Glass Containers Corporation		**Obear-Nester Glass Company**		**Anchor Hocking Glass Corp.**	
Antioch, CA	25	East St. Louis, IL	39	Connellsville, PA	10
Los Angeles, CA	26			Los Angeles, CA	11
		Owens-Illinois		Jacksonville, FL	57
Glenshaw Glass Company, Inc.		Alton, IL	41		
Glenshaw, PA	28	Bridgeton, NJ	42	**Armstrong Cork Company**	
		Fairmont, WV	43	Millville, NJ	13
Knox Glass, Inc.		Huntington, WV	44		
Jackson, MS	30	Streator, IL	45	**Ball Brothers Company**	
Palestine, TX	31	Waco, TX	46	El Monte, CA	16
Parker, PA	32	Clarion, PA	47	Okmulgee, OK	17
		Oakland, CA	49		
Latchford-Marble Glass Co.		Los Angeles, CA	50	**Brockway Glass Company, Inc.**	
Los Angeles, CA	33			Brockway, PA	18
		Reed Glass Company		Muskogee, OK	19
Laurens Glass Works, Inc.		Rochester, NY	52		
Laurens, SC	35			**Buck Glass Company**	
		Thatcher Glass Mfg. Co., Inc.		Baltimore, MD	21
Liberty Glass Company		Elmira, NY	54		
Sapulpa, OK	37	Streator, IL	55	**Chattanooga Glass Company**	
		Saugus, CA	56	Chattanooga, TN	23

117

Bottles

This is a general guide to Pepsi-Cola bottles and prices. It is not intended to be an in-depth guide, but only to give an overview of prices and dates of Pepsi bottles. There are other books on the market that are dedicated strictly to Pepsi bottles.

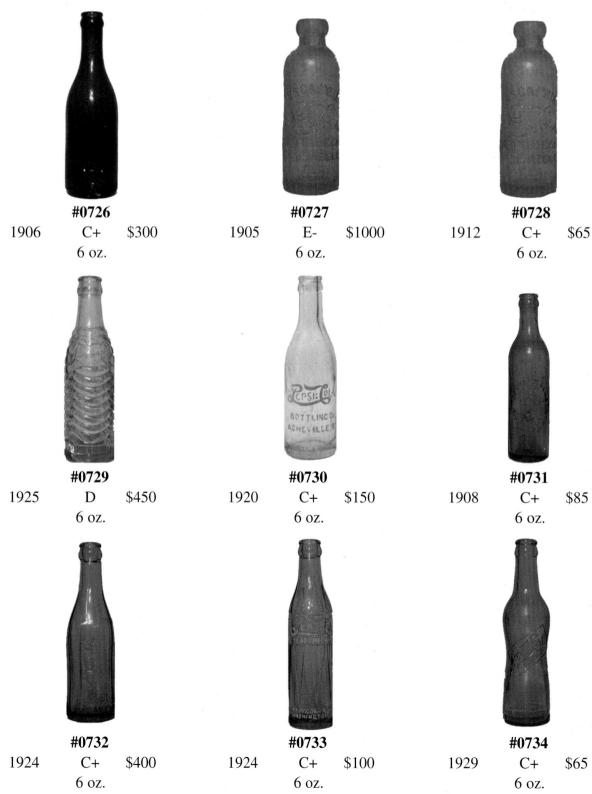

#0726			**#0727**			**#0728**		
1906	C+	$300	1905	E-	$1000	1912	C+	$65
6 oz.			6 oz.			6 oz.		
#0729			**#0730**			**#0731**		
1925	D	$450	1920	C+	$150	1908	C+	$85
6 oz.			6 oz.			6 oz.		
#0732			**#0733**			**#0734**		
1924	C+	$400	1924	C+	$100	1929	C+	$65
6 oz.			6 oz.			6 oz.		

#0735

1934   E $500

12 oz.

#0736

1940   D $125

12 oz.

#0737

1939   D $150

12 oz.

#0738

1939   D $150

12 oz.

#0739

1940   C+ $75

12 oz.

#0740

1943   C+ $50

12 oz.

#0741

1945   C+ $10

12 oz.

#0742

1947   B $5

12 oz.

#0743

1945   C+ $50

12 oz.

#0744

1951   B $5

12 oz.

#0745

1948   C $25

12 oz.

#0746

1958   A $5

12 oz.

#0747

1928	D	$400
24 oz.		

#0748

1945	C+	$100
32 oz.		

#0749

1951	C+	$100
32 oz.		

#0750

1951	D+	$150
32 oz.		

#0751

1951	C+	$100
32 oz.		

#0752

1965	C+	$45
32 oz.		

#0753

1969	B	$10
26 oz.		

#0754

1970	B	$10
32 oz.		

#0755

1958	A	$10
26 oz.		

#0756

1978   A $5

32 oz.

#0757

1977   A $5

1 liter

#0758

1976   B $10

64 oz.

#0759

1970   E $350

16 oz.

#0760

1975   D $35

10 oz.

#0761

1971   C+ $20

16 oz.

#0762

1949   C+ $65

6 oz. no return

#0763

1951   D+ $125

7 oz. no return

#0764

1965   A $5

16 oz. no return

#0765

1960 C $500

20" tall

#0766

1940 E $1000

32 oz.

#0767

1977 C+ $50

12 oz. Special Bottle

#0768

1973 C+ $100

Anniversary Bottle 6 oz.

#0769

1972 D $35

12 oz.

#0770

1998 E $250

Tiffany 100th Anniversary

#0771

1998 A $5

12 oz.

#0772

1998 A $5

12 oz.

#0773

1998 A $5

12 oz.

#0774

1998 A $5

12 oz.

COMMEMORATIVE BOTTLES

The Pepsi commemorative bottle era began in the 1970s. Although there were some commemorative bottles issued prior to that time, those were mostly produced for internal awards and events, and were not widely distributed. The commemorative bottles produced from the 1970s on were produced in the hundreds of thousands. For this reason, very few of them have achieved any significant value. Most of these commemorative bottles can be purchased for between $5 and $15. This does not diminish their importance as collectibles. The events these bottles commemorate make these bottles worthy of collecting.

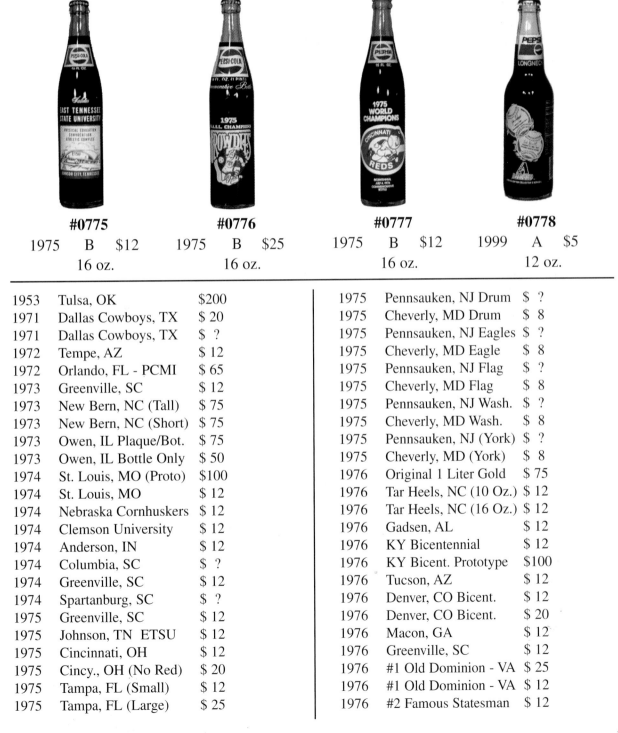

#0775	#0776	#0777	#0778
1975 B $12	1975 B $25	1975 B $12	1999 A $5
16 oz.	16 oz.	16 oz.	12 oz.

1953	Tulsa, OK	$200	1975	Pennsauken, NJ Drum	$?
1971	Dallas Cowboys, TX	$ 20	1975	Cheverly, MD Drum	$ 8
1971	Dallas Cowboys, TX	$?	1975	Pennsauken, NJ Eagles	$?
1972	Tempe, AZ	$ 12	1975	Cheverly, MD Eagle	$ 8
1972	Orlando, FL - PCMI	$ 65	1975	Pennsauken, NJ Flag	$?
1973	Greenville, SC	$ 12	1975	Cheverly, MD Flag	$ 8
1973	New Bern, NC (Tall)	$ 75	1975	Pennsauken, NJ Wash.	$?
1973	New Bern, NC (Short)	$ 75	1975	Cheverly, MD Wash.	$ 8
1973	Owen, IL Plaque/Bot.	$ 75	1975	Pennsauken, NJ (York)	$?
1973	Owen, IL Bottle Only	$ 50	1975	Cheverly, MD (York)	$ 8
1974	St. Louis, MO (Proto)	$100	1976	Original 1 Liter Gold	$ 75
1974	St. Louis, MO	$ 12	1976	Tar Heels, NC (10 Oz.)	$ 12
1974	Nebraska Cornhuskers	$ 12	1976	Tar Heels, NC (16 Oz.)	$ 12
1974	Clemson University	$ 12	1976	Gadsen, AL	$ 12
1974	Anderson, IN	$ 12	1976	KY Bicentennial	$ 12
1974	Columbia, SC	$?	1976	KY Bicent. Prototype	$100
1974	Greenville, SC	$ 12	1976	Tucson, AZ	$ 12
1974	Spartanburg, SC	$?	1976	Denver, CO Bicent.	$ 12
1975	Greenville, SC	$ 12	1976	Denver, CO Bicent.	$ 20
1975	Johnson, TN ETSU	$ 12	1976	Macon, GA	$ 12
1975	Cincinnati, OH	$ 12	1976	Greenville, SC	$ 12
1975	Cincy., OH (No Red)	$ 20	1976	#1 Old Dominion - VA	$ 25
1975	Tampa, FL (Small)	$ 12	1976	#1 Old Dominion - VA	$ 12
1975	Tampa, FL (Large)	$ 25	1976	#2 Famous Statesman	$ 12

1976	St. Louis Arch Proto.	$125
1976	New Bern, NC	$ 12
1976	Miami, OH Erie Canal	$ 12
1976	Ft. Amanda/Finley, OH	$ 12
1976	Ohio - Appleseed	$ 50
1976	Ohio - Appleseed	$ 12
1976	Anderson, SC	$ 12
1976	Fort Wayne, IN	$125
1976	Mtn. State - WV	$ 12
1976	Famous Places - WV	$ 12
1977	Safford, AZ	$ 12
1977	Iowa Vs. Iowa State	$ 12
1977	OK City, OK	$ 75
1978	Iowa Vs. Iowa State	$ 12
1978	Iowa Vs. ISU (Green)	$ 12
1978	Vancouver, B.C.	$ 40
1979	Greenville, NC (Dew)	$ 30
1979	Bennettsville, SC	$ 60
1979	Memphis, MO	$100
1980	Charlotte, NC	$ 12
1980	Anderson, SC	$ 12
1980	Bennettsville, SC	$ 12
1980	Charleston, SC	$ 12
1980	Columbia, SC	$ 12
1980	Conway, SC	$ 12
1980	Florence, SC	$ 12
1980	Greenville, SC	$ 12
1980	Spartanburg, SC	$ 12
1980	Rio Piedras, P.R.	$ 10
1980	Rio Piedras, P.R.	$ 10
1981	Marshall Vs. Army	$ 25
1982	Bainbridge, GA	$ 40
1982	Tulsa, OK	$ 15
1983	Saluki Pride, IL	$ 12
1983	Saluki Pride (Green)	$?
1983	Fresno, CA	$ 12
1983	Connersville, IN	$ 12
1983	Charlottesville 75	$ 15
1983	Cincinnati, OH	$100
1984	UI Rose Bowl	$ 20
1984	Missouri St. Univ.	$ 12
1984	Winston/Salem, NC	$ 25
1984	Jackson, MS	$100
1984	Jackson, MS (No Red)	$125
1984	Portsmouth, OH	$ 75
1986	Mt. Vernon, OH	$ 40
1986	NC 50th Anniversary	$ 60
1986	Tenn. Homecoming	$ 15
1986	Denver, CO 50th Ann.	$ 30
1986	Moultrie, GA	$ 15

1988	Nashville, TN	$ 25
1988	Charlotte, NC	$ 12
1988	Moultrie, GA	$ 15
1990	Dollywood, TN	$ 15
1990	Philadelphia, PA	$ 15
1990	Philadelphia, PA -Diet	$ 20
1990	Batavia, NY	$ 20
1990	Ray Charles	$?
1991	Columbia, SC - Petty	$ 6
1991	Columbia, SC 7 Time	$ 6
1991	Columbia, SC 200 Wn.	$ 6
1991	100th Nascar Start	$ 6
1991	Bakersfield, CA	$ 8
1991	Dollywood, TN	$ 12
1991	Dollywood, TN	$ 15
1991	Georgia So. Eagles	$ 15
1991	Bainbridge, GA	$ 15
1991	Wenatchee, WA	$ 60
1991	1st Winston Cup Race	$ 4
1991	Most. Conseq. Wins	$ 4
1991	Most Wins in Season	$ 4
1991	Most Poles in Career	$ 4
1991	Most Popular Driver	$ 4
1991	200 Career Victories	$ 4
1991	1st Winston Cup Vict.	$ 4
1991	Petty's Final Year	$ 4
1992	1987 Stars & Stripes	$ 6
1992	1988 Stars & Stripes	$ 6
1992	1992 Stars & Stripes	$ 12
1993	Houston, TX	$ 8
1993	Knoxville, IA	$ 8
1993	Vancouver, BC	$ 15
1993	Vancouver, BC	$ 15
1993	Shaq - Chillin	$ 4
1993	Shaq - Stuffin	$ 4
1993	Shaq - Scorin	$ 4
1993	Shaq - Spinnin	$ 4
1993	Shaq - Slammin	$ 4
1993	Shaq - Jammin	$ 4
1994	Albq. Air Balloon	$ 8
1994	San Jose Sharks	$ 8
1994	Spartansburg, SC	$ 8
1994	Kissimmee, FL	$ 12
1995	Modesto, CA	$ 8
1995	Kissimmee, FL	$ 8

#0779

1991   C $75

Petty Display Set

#0780

1991   E $500

Silver Dipped Petty Set

#0781

1992   C $35

America's Cup Set

#0782

1998   D $300

100th Anniversary Set

#0783

1998   B $25

100th Anniversary 4 Pack

#0784

1996   B+ $10

AZ Diamondbacks 4 Pack

LABELS

These are the most common labels used by the Pepsi-Cola Company in the last 100 years. There were many other labels produced bearing minor differences, such as the addition of the name of the franchise where the Pepsi was bottled.

Finding an intact label is a rare occurrence. Most of these labels were destroyed during use. There are a number of reproduction labels being sold as authentic by unscrupulous dealers.

#0785

1905   E $800

#0786

1939   D $75

#0787

1940   C+ $25

#0788

1941   C $25

#0789

1943   C+ $15

#0790

1969   B $5

#0791

1973   B $5

#0792

1939   D $35

Neck Label

#0793

1940   C+ $30

Neck Label

#0794

1943   C+ $25

Neck Label

#0795

1949　　　E　　$1000

12 oz.

#0796

1950　　　C+　　$300

12 oz.

#0797

1951　　　C+　　$200

12 oz.

#0798

1960　　　B　　$10

12 oz.

#0799

1969　　　E　　$150

12 oz.

#0800

1971　　　B　　$5

12 oz.

#0801

1973　　　B+　　$10

12 oz.

#0802

1976　　　B　　$5

12 oz.

#0803

1979　　　A　　$5

16.9 oz.

#0804

1971   C+ $20

8 oz.

#0805

1985   B $25

12 oz.

#0806

1985   C+ $25

16.9 oz.

COMMEMORATIVE AND CONTEST CANS

Over the last thirty years, Pepsi-Cola has produced hundreds of millions of commemorative cans. They have also produced almost as many to promote contests. One example is the Jackson's Victory Tour can. This can was distributed nationwide, with over 50 million produced. Consequently, almost every collector has a Jackson Victory Tour can and, as a result, there is very little monetary value to this can.

Collecting commemorative cans is quite popular, due to the low cost and availability of the cans. One thing to keep in mind while collecting cans is that they must be drained. Any soft drink can stored over a period of time will eventually begin to leak. It is recommended that you carefully poke holes in the bottom of cans and drain, rather than opening and draining from the top. Most can collectors feel this is an acceptable way to preserve the value of the can.

#0807

1988   A $2

12 oz.

#0808

1995   A $2

12 oz.

#0809

1976   A $2

12 oz.

#0810

1991   D $25

6" x 4" x 4"

#0811

1999   D $100

Destiny Can

#0812

1999   C+ $35

Gold Yoda Can

#0813

1991   A $10

12" x 12" x 3"

#0814

1950   E $500

3 Pack

#0815

1965   D $50

6 Pack

#0816

1965   C $200

12" x 10"

#0817

1973   C+ $35

6 Pack

#0818

1950   E $150

Cardboard Box

#0819

1990   C+ $25

11" x 16" x 8"

#0820

1991   C $50

14" x 6" x 4"

#0821

1991   A $15

18" x 7" x 3"

#0822

1990   D $45

12" x 6" x 6"

#0823

1994   C+ $45

36" Tall

#0824

1994   A $15

16" x 6" x 6"

#0825

1999   D+ $100

11" x 6" x 3"

#0826 Display Case

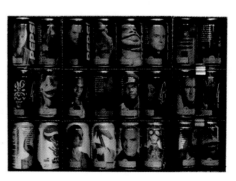

#0826

1999   C+ $75

12" x 15" x 5"

MULTI-BOTTLE PACKAGING

Multi-bottle packaging has become commonplace over the last 50 years. It is hard to imagine that this wasn't always the situation. Original Pepsi-Cola in bottles was sold primarily as a single drink. It wasn't until 1939 that Pepsi-Cola was sold and marketed in a 6-bottle carton. This was a result of the increased availability of ice boxes and electric refrigerators. At this time, a single 12-ounce bottle of Pepsi-Cola sold for a nickel, or a 6-bottle carton for 25 cents. This was the beginning of what has become known as the "take-home" market. From 1939 to the present, multi-bottle and can packaging has mushroomed. The multi-container packaging has consisted of 2-packs, 4-packs, 6-packs, 8-packs, 12-packs, and 24-packs. The material used for packaging Pepsi bottles and cans has included paper, cardboard, cloth, metal, wood, and plastic. As the public's thirst has increased, so has the need for more convenient ways to get Pepsi home to the consumers.

#0827

1939   D $75

6 Bottles

#0828

1940   D $75

6 Bottles

#0829

1940   D $75

6 Bottles

#0830

1940   C+ $50

6 Bottles

#0831

1942   D $65

6 Bottles

#0832

1942   C+ $45

6 Bottles

#0833

1945   C+ $45

6 Bottles

#0834

1945   D $75

6 Bottles

#0835

1945   C+ $45

6 Bottles

#0836

1945   C+ $45

6 Bottles

#0837

1945   C+ $45

6 Bottles

#0838

1945   C+ $45

6 Bottles

#0839

1950   C+ $45

6 Bottles

#0840

1951   C+ $35

12 Bottles

#0841

1951   B $10

6 Bottles

#0842

1954   C $20

12 Bottles

#0843

1960   B $5

6 Bottles

#0844

1963   B $5

8 Bottles

#0845

1956   C+ $35

2 Bottles

#0846

1969   D $15

6 Bottles

#0847

1969   B $5

6 Bottles

#0848

1979   A $2

6 Bottles

#0849

1943   C+ $65

Cloth 6 Bottles

PAPER CARRIERS

During the late 1930s and early 1940s, these paper bag carriers were quite popular. They were basically disposable Pepsi carriers. Due to the weight of the bottles, these carriers did not last more than a few trips.

During World War II, the use of paper carriers was necessary due to material shortages.

#0850

1939   E $100

Paper 6 Bottles

#0851

1940   C+ $85

Paper 6 Bottles

#0852

1939   E $75

Paper 6 Bottles

#0853

1940   C+ $75

Paper 6 Bottles

#0854

1940   D $75

Paper 6 Bottles

#0855

1940   C+ $75

Paper 6 Bottles

#0856

1940   D $75

Paper 6 Bottles

#0857

1945   D $75

Paper 6 Bottles

#0858

1945   C+ $75

Paper 6 Bottles

#0859

1945   E $100

Paper 6 Bottles

#0860

1940   D $125

Cardboard 24 Bottles

#0861

1945   D $125

Cardboard 24 Bottles

#0862

1945   D $100

Cardboard 24 Bottles

#0863

1947   B $35

Cardboard 12 Bottles

#0864

1950   C+ $75

Cardboard 24 Bottles

#0865

1940   C+ $175

Wood 6 Bottles

#0866

1940   C+ $175

Wood 6 Bottles

#0867

1940   E $225

Masonite 6 Bottles

#0868

1940   D $100

Wood 6 Bottles

#0869

1940   C+ $65

Wood 12 Bottles

#0870

1910   D+ $100

Wood 24 Bottles

#0871

1910   E $125

Wood 24 Bottles

#0872

1940   C+ $35

Wood 24 Bottles

#0873

1940   C $25

Wood 24 Bottles

#0874

1945   C+ $45

Wood 24 Bottles

#0875

1951   B $15

Wood 24 Bottles

#0876

1936   D $85

Wood 24 Bottles

#0877

1939   D- $75

Wood 24 Bottles

#0878

1940   C+ $65

Wood 24 Bottles

#0879

1945   C+ $55

Wood 24 Bottles

#0880

1940   C+ $65

Wood 24 Bottles

#0881

1951   B $20

Wood 24 Bottles

RAILROAD SHIPPING CASE

Wood cases such as #0882 were used to ship bottles of Pepsi-Cola to retail customers via the railroad. The customer was responsible for returning the bottles and cases. There are only a few of these cases known to exist today.

#0882

1909   D $150

Wood 48 Bottles

#0883

1940   D $150

Metal 12 Bottles

#0884

1940   D $150

Metal 12 Bottles

#0885

1945   C+ $95

Metal 12 Bottles

#0886

1940   D $125

Metal 6 Bottles

#0887

1940   D $65

Metal 6 Bottles

#0888

1947   B+ $35

Metal 6 Bottles

#0889

1947   A $25

Metal 6 Bottles

#0890

1947   C $65

Metal 6 Bottles

#0891

1951   B+ $25

Metal 6 Bottles

#0892

1965   B $20

Metal 6 Bottles

#0893

1965   B $20

Metal 6 Bottles

#0894

1965   B $10

Plastic 6 Bottles

#0895

1971   B $10

Plastic 6 Bottles

#0896

1951   C+ $15

Grocery Cart Bottle Holder

#0897

1951   C+ $15

2 Bottle Holder

#0898

1940   C+ $60

Metal 24 Bottle

These two items are vendor
bottle carriers, used at ballparks
and other outdoor concessions.

#0899

1951   C+ $45

Metal 24 Bottle

Picnic cooler #0900 was originally art on the cover of a *Pepsi World* magazine. After the bottlers received their magazines, they requested that Pepsi actually produce this picnic cooler. In 1965, it was made available to Pepsi bottlers and the public.

#0900
1965   C+ $35
13" tall

#0901
1965   C $50
13" tall

#0902
1969   B+ $20
13" tall

#0903
1954   B+ $20
9" tall

#0904
1945   C $45
10" x 11"

#0905
1940   D $200
16" tall

#0906
1940   C+ $75
20" x 14"

#0907
1948   C $125
18" x 18"

#0908

1948   C $125

18" x 12"

#0909

1948   C $125

18" x 18"

#0910

1945   D $200

14" x 12"

#0911

1951   C $95

18" x 12"

#0912

1951   C $100

18" x 18"

#0913

1951   C $95

18" x 12"

#0914

1951   C $95

18" x 12"

#0915

1960   C- $45

20" x 14"

#0916

1960   C+ $75

16" x 18"

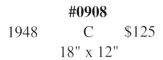

ICE COOLERS

Before the invention of electric refrigeration, stores that sold cold bottles of Pepsi-Cola relied on these types of ice coolers. The major drawback to this type of cooler was the constant need to replace the ice.

#0917

1929   E+ $2000

31" x 33"

#0918

1934   D+ $1200

31" x 33"

Utility Cooler and Stand

#0919

1940   D+ $800

20" x 13"

#0920

1940   D $800

27" x 15"

#0921

1940   D+ $200

25" x 30"

#0922

1939   E $1500

31" x 33"

#0923

1951   E $500

31" x 33"

#0924

1941   E $1800

Salesman's Sample

SALESMAN'S SAMPLE

The item on the right is a salesman's sample - a miniature version of an actual Pepsi cooler. It was used to show customers what the cooler looked like, and was very often given out to customers who placed large orders.

ELECTRIC COOLERS

In 1940, Pepsi began using electric coolers. These new coolers worked by circulating cold water through the internal container. These coolers were notorious for causing the paper labels to come off the bottles. Eventually these water coolers were replaced by air coolers.

Most chest coolers, or flat-top coolers, were also available as vendors. The vendors had a rack inside that held the bottles by the neck. After placing money into the coin mechanism, the bottle slid along this rack to an opening activated by the coin drop.

#0925

1940   D+ $1500

34" x 45"

#0926

1941   E $800

44" x 35"

#0927

1945   C+ $600

44" x 35"

#0928
1951　　D　　$2000
24" x 52"
Vendolator 27B

#0929
1955　　C　　$500
47" x 33"
Bevco 160

#0930
1955　　D　　$800
30" x 78"
Vendolator VMC302

#0931
1955　　D　　$1000
25" x 52"
Vendolator VMC33

#0932
1955　　D　　$800
27" x 58"
Vendolator 81

#0933
1955 C+ $500
42" x 40"
Ideal 55

#0934
1955 D $500
39" x 72"
United Visi-Cooler P384

#0935
1955 D+ $400
28" x 70"
Premix Vendor

#0936
1965 B+ $250
25" x 52"
Vendolator VFB56

#0937
1975 B+ $200
30" x 70"
Choice Vend CV2-299

#0938

1905   E $75

First Crown

#0939

1923   D $35

#0940

1928   D $25

#0941

1929   C+ $20

#0942

1936   C- $10

#0943

1939   D $20

Promotional Crown

#0944

1941   C $10

#0945

1941   D $20

Promotional Crown

#0946

1951   B $5

#0947

1965   A $2

#0948

1971   A $1

#0949

1991   A $1

#0950

1939   C+ $10

Crown with Tax Stamp

#0951

1945   C+ $15

Crown with Size Mark

#0952

1962   C+ $10

Promotional Contest

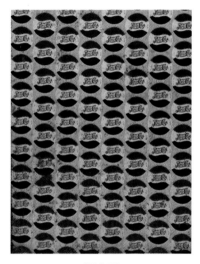

#0953

1945   D $75

Uncut Crowns

CROWNS

Crowns, or bottle caps, have been used by the Pepsi-Cola Company since 1905. At first, they were simply used to seal and mark the bottles. Later on, they became an important part of the promotion of Pepsi-Cola. As early as 1910, crowns were used as tokens to exchange for merchandise. The success of this program spawned other crown redemption programs over the years.

Crowns were also used as pieces in various Pepsi contests. Specially marked crowns were placed on random bottles of Pepsi with prizes or money designated underneath the cork. Many collectors of crowns specialize in collecting these contest bottle caps.

Paper Cup Holders

#0954

1954   B+ $30

Paper 6 Cup Holder

#0955

1960   B $5

Paper 4 Cup Holder

#0956

1943   E $65

12 oz.

#0957

1943   D+ $50

10 oz.

#0958

1945   C+ $15

12 oz.

#0959

1945   C+ $15

8 oz.

#0960

1951   C+ $10

10 oz.

#0961

1960   B $5

10 oz.

#0962

1956   B $5

10 oz.

#0963

1964   B $5

10 oz.

#0964

1967   B $3

10 oz.

#0965

1969   B $3

10 oz.

#0966

1965   B $3

10 oz.

#0967

1979   A $1

16 oz.

Folding Paper Cup

The cup on the left, #0968, is the rarest of all Pepsi cups. Unfortunately, the graphics are quite plain, which inhibits the collector value of this item.

#0968
1910   E+ $100
Folding Paper Cup

Bakelite Cup Holder

Item #0969 is the only known cone cup holder that bears the Pepsi-Cola trademark. Most cone cup holders from this era are generic.

#0969
1943   D $200
Bakelite Cup Holder

#0970
1943   D $40
10 oz.

#0971
1945   C+ $35
10 oz.

#0972
1951   C+ $30
10 oz.

#0973
1964   C $5
10 oz.

#0974
1950   C $10
Sampling Cup

#0975
1951   C $10
Sampling Cup

#0976
1951   C $5
Sampling Cup

#0977
1960   B $3
Sampling Cup

#0978

1905   E+ $12,000

Ceramic 18" tall

1905 DISPENSER

The dispenser on the left is an original Pepsi syrup dispenser used in soda fountains in the early 1900s. Because of the fragile nature of ceramic, not many survive. They are very rare and sought after by collectors. There is no Pepsi collectible coveted more than the original syrup dispenser.

The dispenser on the right was reissued by the Pepsi-Cola Company. It is a limited edition of only 300.

#0979

1983   D+ $1500

Ceramic 18" tall

#0980

1945   E $800

18" tall

The items on this page are all Pepsi syrup dispensers. They dispensed the syrup into a glass, and the carbonated soda was added separately. Modern dispensers mix the two automatically. Number #0980 played the Pepsi jingle as the handle was depressed to dispense syrup.

#0981

1949   C $225

Musical 6" tall

#0982

1945   D $800

20" tall

#0983

1945   D+ $1000

20" tall

#0984

1954   D- $350

20" tall

FOUNTAIN DISPENSERS

In 1934, Pepsi-Cola was reborn with the introduction of the 12-ounce bottle for 5 cents. The success of the 12-ounce bottle caused Pepsi to all but abandon the fountain business. In 1943, it was decided that Pepsi could no longer ignore this important part of the soft drink business. The company's timing could not have been worse. World War II was at its peak. There were severe material shortages, which made it impossible for Pepsi to get a regular supply of modern fountain dispensers. They were forced to re-enter the fountain business with antiquated equipment. For this reason, Pepsi had to resort to the use of hand-operated equipment to dispense Pepsi-Cola at fountains.

Following the war, Pepsi introduced modern fountain equipment to their customers. From 1945 on, Pepsi used fountain equipment that automatically mixed syrup and carbonated water.

#0985
1943   D $500

#0986
1951   C+ $200

#0988
1960   C+ $250

#0987
1960   D $300
24" tall

Reverse of #0986

#0989
1965   D $150
Home Dispenser

FOUNTAIN DRINKING GLASSES

Fountain drinking glasses, decorated with the Pepsi-Cola logo, have been around since 1905. The earliest Pepsi drinking glasses sell for around $1000, and are very hard to find. It wasn't until the 1940s that fountain drinking glasses were issued on a regular basis.

#0990	**#0991**	**#0992**	**#0993**
1949 C+ $45	1943 B+ $20	1951 B+ $10	1951 C+ $20
10 oz.	10 oz.	10 oz.	10 oz.

#0994	**#0995**	**#0996**
1951 C+ $20	1962 B $5	1962 B $5
10 oz.	10 oz.	10 oz.

PROMOTIONAL DRINKING GLASSES

Promotional drinking glasses, or glasses that are to be given away or sold at a reduced price, have been around since the early 1940s. These were designed to enhance the sale of Pepsi-Cola. The first known promotional glass is the Pepsi & Pete glass. These glasses are in great demand by Pepsi collectors. Regretfully, these glasses have been reproduced. A quick way to recognize the reproduction is that they were manufactured by Anchor-Hocking. The original glass was produced by Owens-Illinois.

#0997	**#0997**	This coupon was redeemed for a set of Pepsi & Pete glasses.	**#0998**
1940 D $400			1940 D+ $200
10 oz.	Reverse		Box for Glasses

#0999

1957   D $50

Tulsa, OK

#1000

1961   C $30

Topeka, KS

#1001

1965   B+ $20

New Haven, MO

#1002

1965   C+ $25

Wichita Falls, TX

#1003

1966   C $20

Kremmling, CO

#1004

1966   C+ $25

Birmingham, AL

#1005

1967   C+ $25

Ft. Smith, AR

#1006

1980   B $20

Eau Claire, WI

#1007

1972   C+ $15

Bottler's Convention

#1008

1969   D $30

Bottler's Convention

#1009

1965   D $35

Sales Meeting

#1010

1957   D $35

Sales Meeting

#1011

1959   D $35

Sales Meeting

#1012

1975   D $30

Bottler's Association

#1013

1976   D $30

Bottler's Association

#1014

1973   C+ $15

75th Anniversary

#1015

1983   B $5

12 oz.

#1016

1983   B $5

12 oz.

#1017

1983   B $5

12 oz.

#1018

1983   B $5

12 oz.

#1019

1983   A $3

16 oz.

#1020

1980   A $2

16 oz.

#1021

1980   A $2

12 oz.

#1022

1990   A+ $3

With lid 12 oz.

#1023

1995   E $200

Large Display Glass

#1024

1980   A $1

16 oz.

#1025

1980   A $10

Set of 4 in Box

#1026

1985   A $1

12 oz.

#1027

1973   C+ $150

75th Anniversary Set

CARTOON GLASSES

Most cartoon glasses are fairly common and are priced below $10 each. There are a few exceptions that are quite valuable and rare. There were millions of these glasses produced during the 1970s. The following is a list of the more common glasses.

PEPSI COLLECTOR SERIES 1973 WARNER BROS.

Beaky Buzzard	Porky Pig
Bugs Bunny	Road Runner
Cool Cat	Slow Poke Rodriguez
Daffy Duck	Sylvester
Elmer Fudd	Speedy Gonzales
Foghorn Leghorn	Tasmanian Devil
Henery Hawk	Tweety
Pepe LePew	Wile E. Coyote
Petunia Pig	Yosemite Sam

PEPSI COLLECTOR SERIES 1976 WARNER BROS. ACTION

Beaky/Cool Cat/Kite	Porky/Fishing/Tasmanian Devil/Fish
Bugs/Mirror/Ray Gun/Martian	Porky/Pot/Daffy/Ladle
Cool Cat/Coconut/Hunter	Road Runner/Catapult/Coyote/Rock
Daffy/Elmer/Bugs/Sign	Slow
Daffy/Tasmanian Devil/Fire Cracker	Poke/Speedy/Sylvester/Hammer
Elmer/Bugs/Gun/Carrots	Sylvester/Granny/Tweety/Birdbath
Foghorn/Dog/Dog House/Bomb	Sylvester/Limb/Tweety/Sawing
Hoppy/Sylvester	Sylvester/Tweety/Net/Bulldog
Jr./Sylvester/Boxing	Wile/Sheep/Sheepdog/Rope
Pepe/Cat/Perfume	Wile/Skateboard & Sail/Road Runner
Pepe/Hose/Daffy/Kink	Yosemite/Goldpan/Speedy/Gold
Petunia/Painting/Porky/Mowing	Yosemite/Pirate/Bugs/Cannon

Warner Bros. glasses came in 11.5 oz. and 16 oz. sizes.

#1028
1951   C+ $150
Case of 12 in Box

#1029
1943   C+ $250
Case of 12 in Box

#1030
1945   C+ $250
Case of 12 in Box

PEPSI SYRUP

Pepsi-Cola is made by combining carbonated water and Pepsi syrup. This was done at the bottling plant on a large scale, and at the local soda fountain for a single serving. One ounce of Pepsi syrup was combined with five ounces of carbonated water to produce a glass of Pepsi-Cola.

#1031

1905   E+ $2000

12"

#1032

1909   D+ $1000

1 gallon

#1033

1945   C+ $125

1 gallon

#1034

1945   D+ $50

Cover

#1035

1951   C $100

1 gallon

#1036

1960   B+ $30

1 gallon

#1037

1963   B+ $20

1 gallon

#1038

1954   C $45

1 gallon

#1039

1960   B+ $25

1 gallon

#1040

1964   B+ $25

1 gallon

#1041

1975   B- $20

1 gallon

#1042

1960   C+ $35

Holds 4 syrup jugs

PEPSI CONCENTRATE

Pepsi concentrate is all the ingredients that make Pepsi-Cola syrup, with the exception of water and sugar. Pepsi bottlers buy concentrate from the Pepsi-Cola Company, then mix it with water and sugar to produce Pepsi-Cola syrup. From there, the syrup is either used to bottle Pepsi or sold to fountains that dispense Pepsi.

In the 1930s, Pepsi-Cola concentrate sold for $350 for a 10 gallon barrel like those pictured below.

#1043

1951   D+ $200

5 gallons

Both of these concentrate barrels are 5 gallon barrels. It is very unusual to find concentrate barrels in this size. There are only a few known to exist.

#1044

1945   D+ $225

5 gallons

#1045

1939   D $175

10 gallons

#1046

1940   E $200

10 gallons

#1047

1940   C+ $125

10 gallons

A kit was available to convert these barrels into ice coolers.

#1048

1940   C+ $125

10 gallons

#1049

1947   C+ $150

10 gallons

#1050

1939   E $350

10 gallons

(Side View)

These barrels were used to ship Pepsi concentrate to Pepsi bottlers. Concentrate, when combined with sugar and water, becomes Pepsi syrup. The metal barrels were designed to be used as picnic coolers after the concentrate was used. Pepsi even offered an adapter kit to make it easier to use these as ice coolers.

Novelties, toys, and accessories is the broadest category in this book. It pretty much covers everything that doesn't fit in any of the other sections.

Novelties are relatively inexpensive items that are given away to promote brand recognition and goodwill. Novelty items were commonly given away at plant openings and special events. Some of the more common novelties given away over the years have been pencils, pens, cigarette lighters, ashtrays, and keychains. Items such as cigarette lighters and ashtrays are especially interesting today, in light of the growing trend against smoking—it is unlikely that novelties associated with smoking will be made in the future. Miniature bottles are among the most popular novelties produced. For the most part, they were distributed between 1940 and 1980. Many collectors favor these miniatures because of their detail and realistic appearance. Salt and pepper shakers have been popular novelties for over fifty years. Some may think that these should be fountain items, because they were used in restaurants and other places that served Pepsi. While this is true, the vast majority of salt and pepper shakers were distributed to the public as novelties.

Toys bearing the Pepsi-Cola logos have been produced as far back as the 1930s. In this category, there are two types of toys. The first is toys that were produced for the Pepsi-Cola Company as promotional items. These types of toys are usually the less valuable of the Pepsi toys. One example is the Pepsi bank in the shape of a Pepsi cooler. These were made for the Pepsi-Cola Company, who in turn offered them to their customers for resale to the public. The second type of toys are those licensed by Pepsi-Cola to be manufactured and sold by toy companies. These toys are generally made to a higher standard.

Accessories include an assortment of Pepsi items that bear the Pepsi trademark, and range from ties to umbrellas. Many of these accessories were produced for the Pepsi-Cola Company to use in everyday operations, such as embroidered emblems. Other accessories, such as umbrellas, were used as gifts for customers.

NOVELTIES, TOYS, AND ACCESSORIES

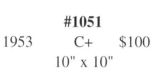

#1051

1953   C+ $100

10" x 10"

#1052

1966   C+ $40

6" x 4"

#1053

1986   C+ $65

9" x 12"

#1054

1974   C+ $50

14" x 12"

#1055

1956   C $35

18" x 12"

#1056

1965   C $75

18" x 20"

#1057

1981   B+ $20

25" x 15"

#1058

1973   C+ $125

12" x 12"

#1059

1983   C+ $125

10" dia.

#1060

1940	D+	$350

5" tall

#1061

1958	D+	$175

5" tall

#1062

1951	D+	$175

12 oz.

#1063

1975	C+	$45

12" tall

#1064

1976	C+	$150

1 liter

#1065

1951	D	$150

Bookends

#1066

1960	C+	$45

4" x 4"

#1067

1973	C+	$100

75th Anniversary

#1068

1976	C+	$20

World Series Ball

#1069

1909   D+ $2500

10" x 18"

#1070

1910   D+ $2500

10" x 18"

#1071

1921   E $1500

14" x 20"

#1072

1939   D $250

7" x 14"

#1073

1939   D+ $500

13" x 16"

#1074

1940   D+ $650

15" x 23"

#1075

1940   D $250

12" x 14"

#1076

1940   D $200

15" x 23"

#1077

1941   C+ $225

15" x 23"

#1078

1941   D+ $300

29" x 43"

#1079

1947   D $150

12" x 15"

#1080

1948   D $500

Rockwell Art 11" x 33"

#1081

1950   D $450

6 Sheets 13" x 22"

#1082

1951   C+ $100

12" x 15"

#1083

1944   E- $400

9" x 12"

#1084

1951   D+ $350

9" x 12"

#1085

1948   D+ $350

6" x 8"

#1086

1956   D- $150

8" x 12"

#1087

1954   C $85

Easel Back 10" x 13"

#1088

1955   C $85

Easel Back 10" x 13"

#1089

1964   C $45

8" x 12"

#1090

1965   C+ $45

8" x 12"

#1091

1969   C $25

6" x 12"

#1092

1969   C $45

20" x 10"

#1093

1970   C $45

20" x 10"

#1094

1973   C $35

9" x 12"

#1095

1980   A $10

10" x 12"

#1096

1942   B $45

17" x 23"

#1097

1943   B $45

17" x 23"

#1098

1944   B $45

15" x 20"

#1099

1945   B $45

15" x 20"

These calendars represent an effort by Pepsi-Cola to support American art. Each year, a nationwide competition was held to find the best American artist. The winning entries became the pages of the calendars for that year. Each year, Pepsi distributed between 500 and 750,000 of these calendars. Although fairly common, these calendars do represent an important part of Pepsi-Cola's history of community outreach.

#1100

1946   B $45

15" x 20"

#1101

1947   B $45

15" x 20"

#1102

1948   B $45

15" x 20"

#1103

1949   B $45

15" x 20"

EMBROIDERED EMBLEMS

Embroidered emblems, also known as patches, were initially used as markings for Pepsi employees and route salesmen. Most of the emblems in this section are that type. In later years, embroidered emblems were produced as souvenirs for Pepsi sponsored events and other special promotions. Today there are very few of these produced, which makes the older emblems more interesting and collectible.

#1104

1940   D+ $45

10"

#1105

1945   C+ $45

7"

#1106

1951   C $25

7"

#1107

1954   C $20

7"

#1108

1963   C   #15

7"

#1109

1971   A $5

9"

#1110

1940   C+ $20

2"

#1111

1940   C+ $20

3"

#1112

1945   C $15

2"

#1113

1951   B $10

3"

#1114

1954   B+ $5

3"

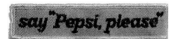

#1115

1960   A $5

4"

#1116

1960   C+ $10

3-1/2"

#1117

1963   C $5

3"

#1118

1963   B $5

3"

#1119

1963   B $5

3"

#1120

1964   A $5

4"

#1121

1964   A+ $5

3"

#1122

1968   C+ $10

2"

#1123

1969   C $10

3"

#1124

1971   A $2

3"

#1125
1973   C+ $20
2-1/2"

#1126
1973   C $10
3-1/2"

#1127
1975   C+ $10
3"

#1128
1978   B $5
3"

#1129
1978   C $5
3"

#1130
1978   C $5
3-1/2"

#1131
1978   A $5
4"

#1132
1978   A $5
3-1/2"

#1133
1980   C+ $5
3-1/2"

#1134
1980   D $20
3"

#1135
1982   A $5
4"

#1136
1991   B $10
3-1/2"

FANS

Fans have been a useful advertising novelty distributed by the Pepsi-Cola Company since the early 1900s. In the days before air conditioning fans were a necessity, especially in public places. Fans were used in movie theaters, churches, restaurants, baseball games and various other community gatherings.

The earliest fans were made of a thin paper-like material that resulted in most of them being lost due to deterioration.

Reverse

#1137

1906   E+ $1800

Paper (Front)

Reverse

#1138

1910   D+ $1800

Cardboard (Front)

#1139

1938   D $125

Cardboard (Front)12" tall

Reverse

#1140

1940   C $125

Cardboard (Front) 11" tall

#1141

1949   D $65

Cardboard (Front)10" tall

Reverse

(Reverse of above)

#1142

1949   D $125

Cardboard (Front)10" tall

Reverse

#1143

1940   D $65

12" tall

#1144
1908   E+ $6500
Back Bar 10" x 13"

#1145
1909   E+ $8000
Strawholder 6" tall

#1146
1908   E+ $250
Strawholder 5" x 4"

#1147
1945   E $1200
7" x 11"

#1148
1949   D+ $550
Metal Back Bar 4"

#1149
1945   D $600
Napkin Hold. 7" x 5"

#1150
1940   D+ $200
Toothpick Holder

#1151
1962   C $35
Toothpick Holder

#1152
1978   B $15
Napkin Holder

#1153

1940   D $125

Plate 11" x 7"

If you sold Pepsi-Cola at your soda fountain or restaurant during the 1940s, these are the types of promotional items the Pepsi-Cola Company might have given you to use in your establishment.

#1154

1943   D+ $650

Straw Holder 10" tall

#1155

1943   D+ $650

Straw Holder 4" x 3"

#1156

1943   D+ $300

Menu Holder 2" tall

#1157

1943   D+ $350

Salt & Pepper 4" tall

#1158

1943   D+ $650

Spoon Holder 6" tall

#1159

1943   D+ $650

Napkin Hold. 7" x 5"

#1160

1945   D $45

Dispenser Handle

#1161

1960   C $15

Dispenser Handle

#1162

1960   C $10

Dispenser Handle

#1163

1960   C $10

Dispenser Handle

#1164

1964   C+ $20

Dispenser Handle

#1165

1987   B $5

Dispenser Handle

#1166

1943   C $15

Fountain Insert

#1167

1940   C $20

Bottle Spout

#1168

1945   B $10

Resealable Cap

#1169
1945   D $100
Money Clip

#1170
1960   C $15
Money Clip

#1171
1955   C+ $20
Money Clip

#1172
1958   C+ $25
Tie Clip

#1173
1964   C $10
Tie Clip

#1174
1978   B $5
Tie Clip

#1175
1960   B $10
Tie Clip

#1176
1940   D $75
Cuff Links

#1177
1945   D $75
Cuff Links

#1178
1965   A $5
Cuff Links

#1179
1951   A $5
Button

#1180
1941   C $65
Medal

#1181
1972   A $10
Medal

#1182

1940   D $55

Key Chain/Coin Saver

#1183

1951   D $75

Keychain/Flashlight

#1184

1954   D $25

Two View Keychain

#1185

1951   C $15

Keychain

#1186

1951   C+ $20

Keychain

#1187

1951   C $10

Keychain

#1188

1960   B+ $5

Keychain

#1189

1951   C+ $25

Keychain

#1190

1960   C+ $15

Keychain

#1191

1970   B $5

Keychain

#1192

1962   B $5

Keychain

#1193

1962   B $5

Keychain

#1194

1910   D+ $250

Lapel Pin

#1195

1910   E $550

Service Pin

#1196

1942   D $75

Lapel Pin

#1197

1943   D $85

Lapel Pin

#1198

1943   D+ $75

Service Pin

#1199

1943   D+ $75

Service Pin

#1200

1945   C $55

Lapel Pin

#1201

1945   D $55

Lapel Pin

#1202

1945   D+ $75

Service Pin

#1203

1951   D $75

Safety Award Pin

#1204

1953   C+ $65

Service Pin

#1205

1954   C+ $50

Service Pin

#1206

1951   D $65

Service Pin

#1207

1955   D $60

Service Pin

#1208

1951   A $15

Lapel Pin

#1209

1958   C+ $35

Lapel Pin

#1210
1960   C $25
Lapel Pin

#1211
1964   C+ $20
Lapel Pin

#1212
1976   C+ $10
Lapel Pin

#1213
1980   C+ $15
Lapel Pin

#1214
1960   C+ $45
Award Pin

#1215
1970   C $25
Service Pin

#1216
1991   C $35
Service Pin

#1217
1991   C $25
Charm

#1218
1910   D+ $175
Charm

#1219
1945   D $175
Charm

#1220
1910   B+ $175
Charm

#1221
1960   B $10
Charm

#1222
1941   D $100
Stick Pin

#1223
1951   D- $25
Stick Pin

#1224
1945   D $75
Stick Pin

#1225
1940   D $75
Miniature

#1226
1940   C+ $50
Miniature

#1227
1940   C $45
Miniature

#1228
1940   C+ $55
Miniature

#1229
1951   C $10
Miniature

#1230
1951   C $10
Miniature

#1231
1958   B+ $5
Miniature

#1232
1973   A $5
Miniature

#1233
1958   C+ $100
Miniature

#1234
1973   B+ $25
Miniature

#1235
1940   D+ $125
Salt & Pepper

#1236
1940   D $150
Salt & Pepper

#1237
1940   D $175
Salt & Pepper

#1238
1941   C+ $150
Salt & Pepper

#1239
1958   A+ $15
Salt & Pepper

#1240
1973   A $10
Salt & Pepper

#1241

1985   B $15

Digital Clock

#1242

1980   A $35

Telephone

#1243

1978   C+ $100

Telephone

#1244

1967   C $25

License Plate

#1245

1970   B $5

Flashlight

#1246

1948   D $30

Contest Pouch

#1247

1985   D $100

Cell 10" x 8"

#1248

1940   D $150

Glass Slide

#1249

1940   D $45

Wallet

#1250

1940   C+ $45

Sidewalk Marker

#1251

1951   B $10

Ice Pick

#1252

1975   B $5

Belt Buckle

#1253

1910   E $600

Desk Set

#1254

1940   D+ $400

Pencil Holder

#1255

1940   D+ $650

Desk Set

#1256

1945   D $225

Desk Set

#1257

1960   C $50

Paper Weight

#1258

1995   A $35

Commemorative

#1259

1981   C+ $30

Can in Lucite 6" x 4"

#1260

1975   D $45

Convention Commemorative

#1261

1990   D $35

Gift Item

#1262

1939   D- $100

Mystery Knife

#1263

1950   C $25

Pocket Knife

#1264

1950   C $25

Pocket Knife

#1265

1959   C+ $45

Novelty Crown

#1266

1960   C+ $25

Novelty Crown

#1267

1958   B $20

Novelty Crown

#1268

1909   E $250

Shoeshine Brush

#1269

1951   C+ $15

Shoeshine Brush

#1270

1940   D $45

Sewing Kit

#1271

1954   B $10

Sewing Kit

#1272

1950   C $10

Sewing Kit

#1273

1964   B $5

Sewing Kit

#1274

1967   C+ $45

Change Plate

#1275

1967   C+ $45

Change Plate

#1276

1968   C+ $45

Change Plate

#1277

1965   C $25

Change Mat

#1278

1960   C+ $35

Change Mat

#1279

1975   B+ $10

Grocery Divider

#1280

1970   B+ $10

Grocery Divider

#1281

1955   D $100

Door Mat

#1282

1975   C $50

Door Mat

#1283

1934   D $55

Wall Mount

#1284

1940   B+ $20

Wall Mount

#1285

1940   D $85

Wall Mount

#1286

New   A $10

Wall Mount

#1287

1940   C $35

Metal

#1288

1943   D $45

Plastic Handle

#1289

1940   C+ $30

Plastic Handle

#1290

1940   D- $45

Plastic Handle

#1291

1936   D- $40

Metal

#1292

1939   C+ $25

Metal

#1293

1940   C $10

Metal

#1294

1920   D $85

Metal

#1295

1940   C+ $30

Plastic Handle

#1296

1920   D $85

Metal

#1297

1920   D $85

Metal

#1298

1940   D $75

Metal

#1299	**#1300**	**#1301**	**#1302**
1940 C $45	1940 C+ $35	1940 C+ $35	1951 B $5
Metal	Metal	Metal	Metal

#1303	**#1304**	**#1305**	**#1306**
1951 B $10	1940 D $35	1920 D $65	1930 D $65
Metal	Metal	Metal	Metal

#1307	**#1308**	**#1309**	**#1310**
1960 A $2	1940 B $25	1951 C- $5	1960 B $2
Metal	Metal	Metal	Metal/Plastic

#1311	**#1312**	**#1313**	**#1314**
1970 A $2	1951 B+ $15	1965 B $5	1962 B+ $10
Metal/Plastic	Metal	Metal/Plastic	Metal/Plastic

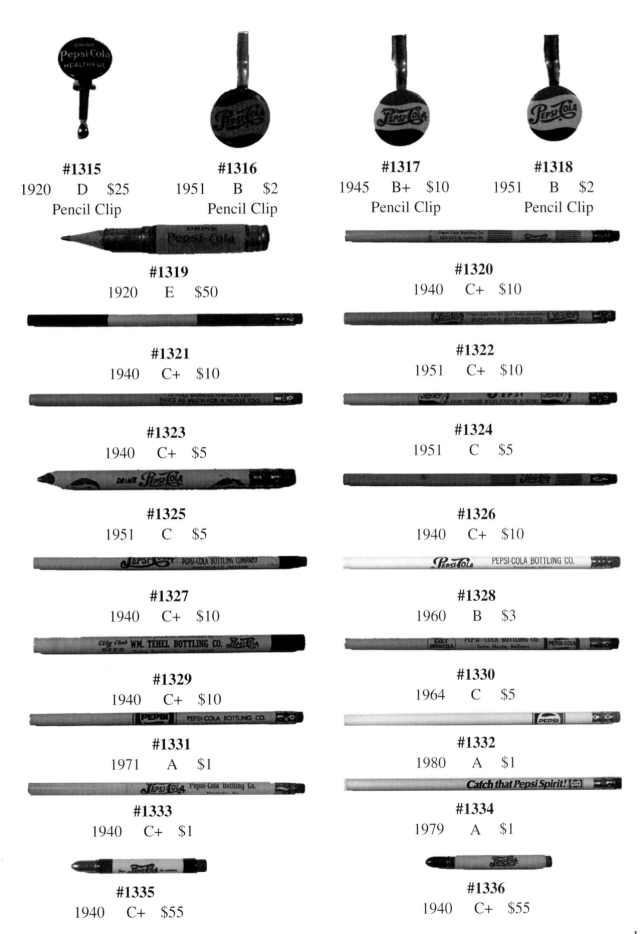

#1315

1920   D $25

Pencil Clip

#1316

1951   B $2

Pencil Clip

#1317

1945   B+ $10

Pencil Clip

#1318

1951   B $2

Pencil Clip

#1319

1920   E $50

#1320

1940   C+ $10

#1321

1940   C+ $10

#1322

1951   C+ $10

#1323

1940   C+ $5

#1324

1951   C $5

#1325

1951   C $5

#1326

1940   C+ $10

#1327

1940   C+ $10

#1328

1960   B $3

#1329

1940   C+ $10

#1330

1964   C $5

#1331

1971   A $1

#1332

1980   A $1

#1333

1940   C+ $1

#1334

1979   A $1

#1335

1940   C+ $55

#1336

1940   C+ $55

#1337

1951   C+ $45

#1338

1940   C+ $55

#1339

1951   C+ $65

#1340

1951   C+ $25

#1341

1940   D $75

#1342

1940   C+ $60

#1343

1940   D $75

#1344

1950   C+ $45

#1345

1940   C+ $60

#1346

1940   C+ $60

#1347

1951   B+ $15

#1348

1951   B+ $25

#1349

1980   B $5

#1350

1970   B+ $10

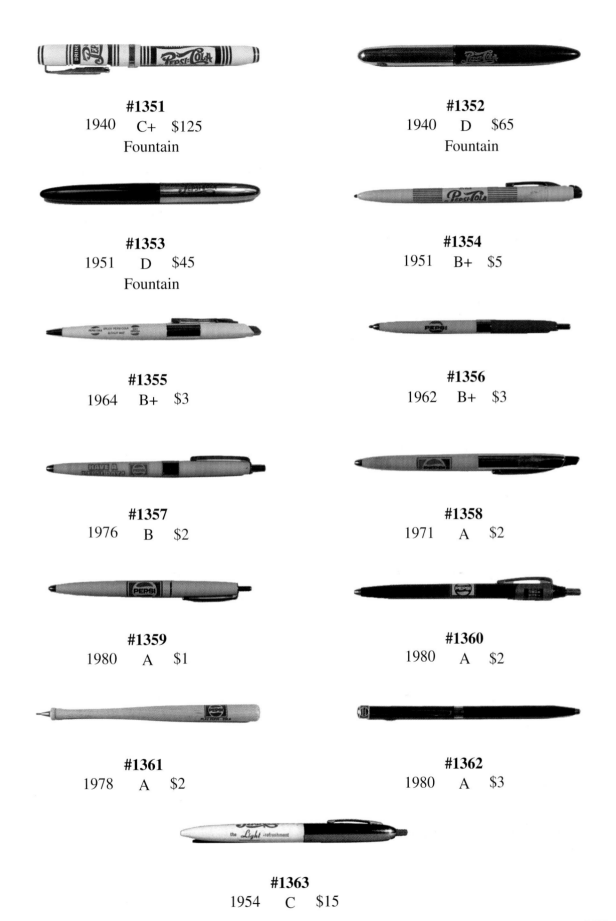

#1351
1940   C+ $125
Fountain

#1352
1940   D $65
Fountain

#1353
1951   D $45
Fountain

#1354
1951   B+ $5

#1355
1964   B+ $3

#1356
1962   B+ $3

#1357
1976   B $2

#1358
1971   A $2

#1359
1980   A $1

#1360
1980   A $2

#1361
1978   A $2

#1362
1980   A $3

#1363
1954   C $15

#1364

1910   E+ $600

#1365

1909   E+ $1000

#1366

1940   E $400

#1367

1940   C+ $35

#1368

1940   D $45

#1369

1940   D $35

#1370

1940   C $20

#1371

1940   C $20

#1372

1943   E $75

#1373

1945   C+ $25

#1374

1947   C $25

#1375

1950   D $30

#1376

1951   D $40

#1377

1951   B $10

#1378

1951   B $10

#1379

1956   C $35

#1380

1956   C $35

#1381

1957   D $65

#1382

1956   C $20

#1383

1958   C $15

#1384

1959   B $5

#1385

1959   C $5

#1386

1960   C+ $30

#1387

1962   C+ $25

#1388

1956   C $15

#1389

1960   C $15

#1390

1964   B $10

#1391

1964   B $10

#1392

1965   C+ $10

#1393

1968   C $10

#1394

1964   C $10

#1395

1965   C $10

#1396

1969   C $10

#1397

1967   B $5

#1398

1972   C $5

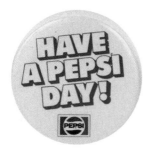

#1399

1976   B $5

#1400

1976   B $3

#1401

1978   A $2

#1402

1978   A $2

#1403

1980   C $10

#1404

1978   C $5

#1405

1979   A $2

#1406

1980   A $2

#1407

1956   C+ $10

#1408

1964   C $10

#1409

1976   B $3

#1410

1978   A $2

#1411

1990   C $5

CONVENTION PINBACK BUTTONS

During the 1950s and early 1960s, Pepsi was engaged in promoting its soft drink at various national events. Free samples of Pepsi-Cola were dispensed at the Republican and Democratic National Conventions. In addition, pinback buttons were given out that featured political themes and Pepsi-Cola. At the Republican Conventions, buttons with elephants were given out. At the Democratic Convention, donkeys were imprinted on the buttons. This program was conducted from 1956 through 1964.

#1412
1956   D $40

#1413
1956   D $40

#1414
1956   D $40

#1415
1956   D $40

#1416
1956   D $40

#1417
1960   D $40

#1418
1964   D $40

#1419
1964   D $40

#1420
1964   C+ $25

#1421
1964   D $40

#1422

1945   D $75

#1423

1942   D $65

#1424

1940   D $45

#1425

1951   C+ $40

#1426

1958   D $85

#1427

1961   C+ $20

#1428

1964   C+ $20

#1429

1964   C+ $20

#1430

1971   C+ $15

#1431
1976   C+ $95

#1432
1976   C+ $95

#1433
1976   C+ $95

#1434
1987   A $5

#1435
1983   A $10

#1436
1980   A $5

#1437
1983   B $10

#1438
1983   A $5

#1439
1980   B $10

#1440
1980   A $5

#1441
1991   A $5

#1442
1958   D $175
Double Set

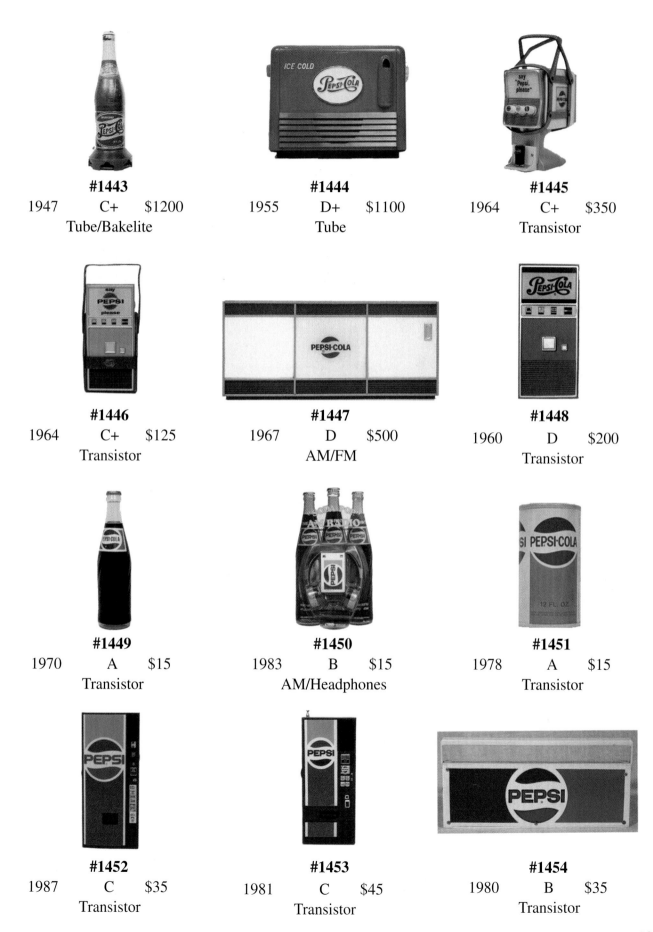

#1443

1947   C+ $1200
Tube/Bakelite

#1444

1955   D+ $1100
Tube

#1445

1964   C+ $350
Transistor

#1446

1964   C+ $125
Transistor

#1447

1967   D $500
AM/FM

#1448

1960   D $200
Transistor

#1449

1970   A $15
Transistor

#1450

1983   B $15
AM/Headphones

#1451

1978   A $15
Transistor

#1452

1987   C $35
Transistor

#1453

1981   C $45
Transistor

#1454

1980   B $35
Transistor

#1455

1943   C+ $55

With Envelope

#1456

1943   C+ $20

With Envelope

#1457

1943   C $15

With Envelope

Envelope

#1458

1969   C+ $10

Promotional

#1459

1961   B $5

Promotional

#1460

1964   B $5

Promotional

#1461

1978   A $3

Promotional

#1462

1971   C+ $5

Convention Gift

#1463

1980   A $5

Promotional

#1464

1960   B $10

Radio Ads

#1465

1965   B $10

Radio Ads

#1466

1965   B $10

Promotional

#1467

1970   B $10

Radio Ads

#1468

1975   B $10

Radio Ads

#1469

1977   B+ $10

Convention Gift

#1470

1976   B $10

Radio Ads

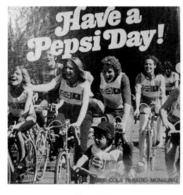

#1471

1977   B $10

Radio Ads

#1472

1986   C $15

Convention Gift

#1473

1940   D $25

Wood

#1474

1940   D $25

Wood

#1475

1945   D $25

Metal

#1476

1951   C $10

Metal

#1477

1954   C $10

Metal

#1478

1960   C+ $10

Metal

#1479

1961   C $10

Metal

#1480

1940   C+ $75

3" x 3"

#1481

1945   C+ $75

3" x 3"

#1482

1950   C+ $55

4" x 4"

#1483

1945   C+ $55

4" dia.

#1484

1945   C+ $75

5" x 5"

#1485

1958   D+ $75

6" x 6"

#1486

1961   D+ $85

6" dia.

#1487

1966   C $25

4" dia.

#1488

1960   C $50

4" x 4"

#1489

1951   C $15

4" x 4"

#1490

1962   C+ $40

5" x 7"

#1491

1965   C+ $45

Plant Opening

199

#1492

1969   C $15

3" x 3"

#1493

1951   C $25

3" dia.

#1494

1951   C+ $35

Ashtray/Lighter

#1495

1940   C+ $45

Cigarette Holder

#1496

1960   B+ $25

Lighter

#1497

1960   C+ $65

Lighter

#1498

1945   C $60

Lighter

#1499

1964   A $10

Lighter

#1500

1976   A $10

Lighter

#1501

1960 D $75

#1502

1954 D $75

#1503

1954 D- $75

#1504

1951 D- $75

#1505

1964 D- $75

#1506

1960 B $15

#1507

1954 B+ $30

#1508

1964 B+ $30

#1509

1964 B+ $30

#1510

1964 B+ $30

#1511

1965 C+ $15

#1512

1960 A $5

#1513

1965 A $10

#1514

1960 A $10

#1515

1951 A $20

#1516

1980 A $10

#1517

1956   C $45

#1518

1976   C $15

#1519

1951   C+ $125
Musical

#1520

1951   D $150
Musical

#1521

1960   C+ $85
Musical

#1522

1961   D $150
Musical

#1523

1940   D $75

#1524

1943   C+ $55

#1525

1951   C $35

#1526

1956   C $20

#1527

1910   E+ $175

#1528

1940   D+ $50

#1529

1939   D- $40

#1530

1939   D- $40

#1531

1939   C+ $15

#1532

1937   C+ $10

#1533

1940   C $5

#1534

1940   C+ $10

#1535

1940   C+ $10

#1536

1940   C $10

#1537

1940   C- $5

#1538

1945   E- $5

#1539

1950   C+ $25

#1540

1950   C+ $25

#1541

1950   C+ $25

#1542

1950   C+ $25

#1543

1950   C $5

#1544

1951   C+ $10

#1545

1951   D $20

#1546

1960   B $5

#1547

1954   B $5

#1548

1961   B $5

#1549

1962   B $3

#1550

1969   B $2

#1551

1971   A $2

DISNEY MATCHBOOKS

Disney and Pepsi-Cola are two of the most collectible trademarks in existence. Combine them and you usually end up with something very special. That's what happened in 1942 when Pepsi and Disney got together to produce matchbooks with military insignias on them. There were 48 different insignias in the complete set. Each matchbook is numbered.

#1552
1942   Set of 48   D $250
Individual Matchbook   C+ $3 each

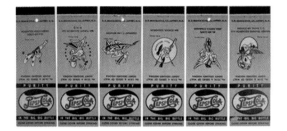

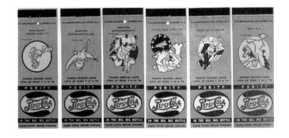

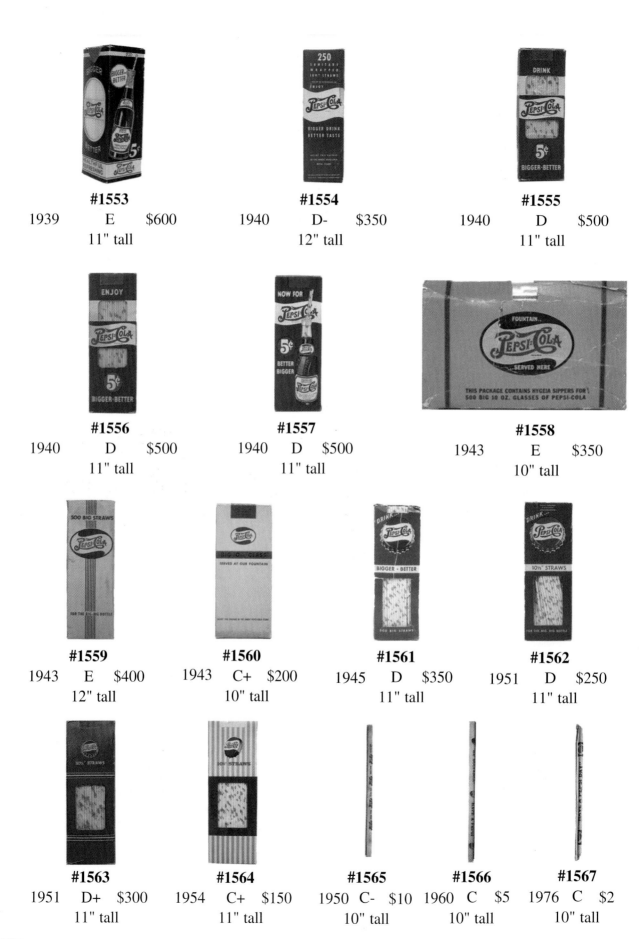

#1553

1939   E $600

11" tall

#1554

1940   D- $350

12" tall

#1555

1940   D $500

11" tall

#1556

1940   D $500

11" tall

#1557

1940   D $500

11" tall

#1558

1943   E $350

10" tall

#1559

1943   E $400

12" tall

#1560

1943   C+ $200

10" tall

#1561

1945   D $350

11" tall

#1562

1951   D $250

11" tall

#1563

1951   D+ $300

11" tall

#1564

1954   C+ $150

11" tall

#1565

1950   C- $10

10" tall

#1566

1960   C $5

10" tall

#1567

1976   C $2

10" tall

#1568

1940   D $45

Necktie

#1569

1960   C $15

Necktie

#1570

1970   A $5

Necktie

#1571

1940   E $250

Apron

#1572

1945   C+ $65

Apron

#1573

1954   C+ $75

Route Salesman Cap

#1574

1954   C+ $10

Felt Hat

#1575

1960   D $35

Plastic

#1576

1960   B $10

#1577

1954   D $150

Toy Pepsi Stand

#1578

1960   C+ $75

Trash Can

#1579

1940   E $150

Flag

#1580

1951   E+ $3000

Scale

#1581

1956   D $200

Folding Chair

#1582

1954   D $200

Folding Chair

#1583

1954   D+ $150

Teepee

#1584

1964   C+ $150

Umbrella

#1585

1951   D $250

Umbrella

#1586

1951   C+ $15

Paper

#1587

1960   C $10

Heavy Paper

#1588

1965   C- $5

Heavy Paper

#1589

1940   C+ $50

Whistle

#1590

1951   C+ $90

Whistle

#1591

1940   D+ $100

Magic Pad

#1592

1950   D $100

Miniature Billboard

#1593

1960   C $25

Miniature Billboard

#1594

1980   B $10

Miniature Billboard

#1595

1976   B $35

26" tall

#1596

1976   C $50

Battery Operated 26" tall

#1597

1940   D $25

Noisemaker

#1598

1960   B $10

Yo-Yo

#1599

1963   B $10

Yo-Yo

#1600

1965   B $10

Yo-Yo

#1601

1988   A $2

Yo-Yo

#1602

1970   A $3

Ball

#1603

1964   C $15

Golf Balls

#1604

1975   C $35

Golf Bag

#1605

1978   B $30

Cake Tin

#1606

1940   D+ $50

Game

#1607

1951   C+ $25

Board Game

#1608

1940   C+ $100

Game

#1609

1940   D $45

Game

#1610

1951   C+ $25

Bingo Card

#1611

1969   B $10

Paper Kite

#1612

1980   B $15

Baseball Bat

#1613

1980   B $45

Musical Dolls

#1614

1960   C+ $150

Miss America Doll

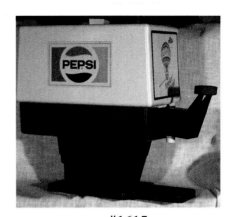

#1615

1970   A $5

Toy Dispenser

#1616

1960   B+ $35

Toy Dispenser

#1617

1960   C+ $125

Playset

#1618

1965   C $45

6' Inflatable

#1619

1960   C $20

12" Inflatable

#1620

1988   A $5

12" Inflatable

#1621

1995   B $15

24" Inflatable

#1622

1940   D $400

Pull Toy

#1623

1956   D $175

Battery Operated

#1624

1945   D $100

Plastic

#1625

1940   C+ $125

Bank

#1626

1940   D $250

Bank

#1627

1960   D+ $600

Bank

#1628

1960   B $25

Bank

#1629

1973   B $10

Bank

#1630

1960   B $20

Bank

#1631

1943   D+ $800

Buddy L Composition 24"

#1632

1950   D+ $500

Plastic 8"

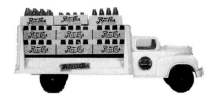

#1633

1950   C+ $275

Marx Plastic 7"

Pictured on the left is a Sears, Roebuck and Co. advertisement featuring truck #1632. In 1950, this toy truck sold for $1.59. What a buy!

#1634

1940   C+ $125

Metal 6"

#1635

1950   D $175

Tin Friction   7"

#1636

1954   D $150

Metal 6"

#1637

1950   D $125

Tin 2"

#1638

1940   D+ $125

Metal 4"

#1639

1945   D $175

Tin Friction 5"

#1640

1954   D $450

Cragsten Metal 11"

#1641

1958   C $300

Ny-Lint Metal 16"

#1642

1951   D $275

Metal Friction 9"

#1643

1963   C+ $250

Metal 4"

#1644

1969   C+ $65

Buddy L Metal 15"

#1645

1951   D+ $175

Metal 4"

#1646

1963   C $50

Metal 2"

#1647

1965   C+ $25

Plastic 2"

#1648

1960   C+ $45

Metal 4"

#1649

1960   B $30

Metal 3.5"

#1650

1978   B $15

Buddy L 10"

#1651

1980   B $10

Matchbox 11"

#1652

1980   B $15

Tonka 14"

#1653

1980   B $10

Matchbox 6"

#1654

1978   B $20

Buddy L Set 10"

#1655

1980   A $35

Ertl 20"

#1656

1985   A $10

Buddy L Set 5"

#1657

1980   A $10

Majorette 10"

#1658

1978   A $10

Tonka 7.5"

#1659

1980   C $35

Ertl 20"

#1660

1978   B- $10

Tootsie 6.5"

#1661

1978   B- $10

Clover Toys 11"

#1662

1982   B $10

Ertl 8"

#1663

1980   A $5

Majorette 6.5"

#1664

1980   A $5

Concur 7.5"

#1665

1978   D $20

Metal 3"

#1666

1980   A $5

3"

#1667

1990   A $10

4"

#1668

1980   A $5

3"

#1669

1978   B $10

3"

#1670

1978   B $5

Friction 3"

#1671

1973   A $5

3"

#1672

1990   A $10

4"

#1673

1980   A $5

3"

#1674

1970   A $5

3"

#1675

1990   A $15

Corgi 3"

#1676

1990   A $20

Corgi 5"

#1677

1980   A $5

Matchbox 3"

#1678

1980   B $20

Corgi 4"

#1679

1945   D $150

9"

#1680

1945   D $100

5"

#1681

1970   D $65

3"

#1682

1975   C $25

7"

#1683

1978   C $35

9"

#1684

1980   C $65

10"

TIP TRAYS

Tip trays are also known as change trays. When a soda fountain patron was presented with a bill, it came on one of these trays. When the bill was paid, the change was placed on these trays. The early trays are very popular with collectors, causing the prices to continually increase.

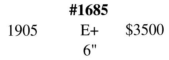

#1685

1905	E+	$3500
	6"	

#1686

1905	E+	$3500
	6"	

#1687

1908	E+	$3800
	6"	

#1688

1909	D	$1200
	6"	

#1689

1910	D	$1200
	6"	

#1690

1906	E	$1500
	6"	

#1691

1951	A	$5
	7" x 5"	

(Reverse of #1691)

TRAYS

Trays are one of the oldest and most consistently used promotional items in the soft drink industry. Early Pepsi trays are among the most sought after collectibles by collectors of Pepsi and advertising memorabilia. Due to their popularity, the prices of the early trays are constantly increasing.

#1692

1908   E $4000
14"

#1693

1909   D+ $1800
14"

#1694

1910   D+ $1800
14"

#1695

1939   D+ $750
12" dia.

Tray #1695 was made for the Giering Bottling Company of Youngstown, Ohio. It was the first known tray to be issued by an individual bottler. For this reason, there was only a small quantity of trays produced, unlike the other Pepsi trays that were distributed nationally.

#1696

1939   D $650
14" x 11"

#1697

1940   C+ $100
14" x 11"

#1698

1940   A $25
14" x 11"

#1699

1940   A $25
14" x 11"

#1700

1950   C+ $250

10" x 14"

#1701

1945   C+ $225

13" dia.

#1702

1955   A $20

12" dia.

#1703

1967   B $35

12" x 12"

#1704

1987   A $20

14" x 12"

New Haven, MO

#1705

1984   C $45

15" x 11"

Zanesville, OH

#1706

1973   B $25

14" x 11"

#1707

1976   A $15

14" dia.

#1708

1973   B $25

12" x 12"

#1693

1909   D+ $1800

Original

#1709

1973   B $20

Reproduction

#1710

1983   A $10

Reproduction

Pepsi-Cola was originally sold at soda fountains, which made serving trays an ideal way to promote and advertise the drink. To make these trays appealing, beautiful girls were used. One such girl on the 1909 tray is referred to as the "Gibson girl." This is in reference to a style of woman used in advertising created by the famous illustrator Charles Dana Gibson. The woman of the 1909 tray may *look* like a Gibson girl, but there is no evidence that this artwork was done by Mr. Gibson. Pictured above is the original 1909 tray along with two reproductions. The key to distinguishing the differences in these trays is by their physical characteristics.

A) The original 1909 tray measures from top to bottom 13-9/16", and from side-to-side 11-1/4". These measurements were made at the widest points. Below the Pepsi-Cola script near the border is the manufacturer name "Niagara Buffalo." The edge of the tray has a light green rolled rim. The back of the tray is painted olive drab.

B) The 1973 reproduction was made as a memento for the 75th anniversary of Pepsi-Cola. From top to bottom it measures 12-5/16" and from side to side it measures 10-1/8". The rolled rim is white and the back of the tray is black.

C) This is from 1983, and is the more recent reproduction of the 1909 tray—and the most common. It measures 14-1/2" from top to bottom and 11-9/16" from side to side. The rim and back are both metallic gold. On the back, the manufacturer name appears - "Fabcraft Inc., Frenchtown, NJ, Made in USA."

The 1973 reproduction tray was originally sold nationwide through newspaper and magazine ads. The tray was part of a set that included the tray and six glasses for $2.95. The offer was good from May of 1973 through March of 1974.

The 1908 tray has also been reproduced. The original size is close to that of the original tray. The reproduction tray is close to the size of the tray described in "C."

Be careful when buying the early Pepsi trays. There have been numerous accounts of buyers being misled regarding the authenticity of their Pepsi trays. Spending several thousand dollars for a reproduction can be devastating. Remember to get a guarantee of authenticity in writing.

#1711

1940   D $85

Cloth

#1712

1940   D $85

Canvas

#1713

1940   D $85

Cloth

#1714

1940   D $75

Cloth

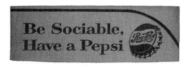

#1715

1960   B $15

Paper

#1716

1958   B $15

Paper

#1717

1960   B $10

Paper

#1718

1963   B $10

Paper

#1719

1967   B $5

Paper

#1720

1975   A $5

Paper

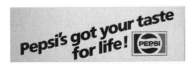

#1721

1981   A $3

Paper

#1722

1983   A $3

Paper

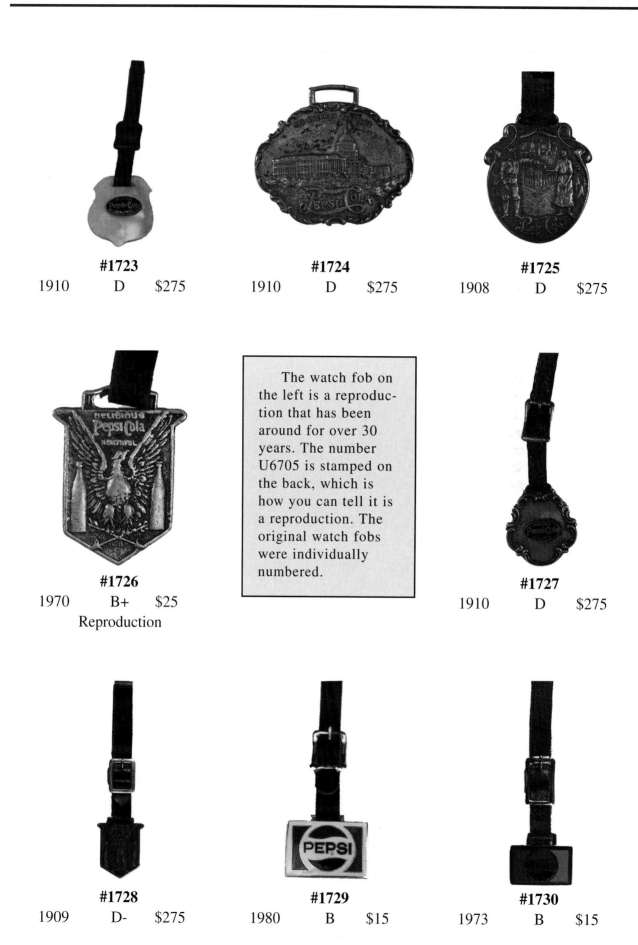

#1723

1910   D $275

#1724

1910   D $275

#1725

1908   D $275

#1726

1970   B+ $25

Reproduction

The watch fob on the left is a reproduction that has been around for over 30 years. The number U6705 is stamped on the back, which is how you can tell it is a reproduction. The original watch fobs were individually numbered.

#1727

1910   D $275

#1728

1909   D- $275

#1729

1980   B $15

#1730

1973   B $15

All companies generate volumes of printed material. The Pepsi-Cola Company is no exception. Over the last one hundred years, the Pepsi-Cola Company, its bottlers, suppliers, and other affiliated companies have created millions of paper items. This includes documents, letters, brochures, internal publications, and other paper items needed to run a company that sells consumer products.

Included in this section is everything from coupons to postcards, from historically important documents to everyday advertisements. To many, these paper items may seem the least important of Pepsi collectibles, but the opposite is true. The documents, advertising books, brochures, and other paper items of the Pepsi-Cola Company are invaluable in determining what and when Pepsi items were produced. Beyond that, these items have helped with identification, dating, and understanding when and why trademarks have changed. It is because of the items in this section that we know as much as we do about the memorabilia of the Pepsi-Cola Company.

Besides the usefulness of these items, there is intrinsic value in owning letters and other documents created by the entrepreneurs who built the Pepsi-Cola Company. There is no other part of Pepsi-Cola collecting that is as exciting as finding old documents that shed new light on the history and the memorabilia of the Pepsi-Cola Company.

PAPER

Blotters

Blotters have gone the way of the fountain pen. Once a necessity on every desk, the invention of the ballpoint pen made these obsolete. Blotters were made of heavy paper and used to blot ink from fountain pens. This makes these collectibles rare and valuable.

#1731

1905   D $175

10" x 4"

#1732

1905   D $175

#1733

1905   E $250

10" x 4"

#1734

1905   D $200

10" x 4"

#1735

1929   D $200

7" x 4"

#1736

1940   B+ $75

9" x 4"

#1737

1940   C+ $125

7" x 4"

#1738

1940   C+ $125

7" x 4"

#1739

1943   D $175

7" x 4"

#1740

1945   C $75

7" x 4"

#1741

1943   C $45

Booklets
Booklets like these were given out to Pepsi consumers as early as 1914. Tens of thousands were distributed, but only a relatively small quantity survived.

#1742
1917   C+ $45
Notebook/Calendar

#1743
1918   C+ $55
Notebook/Calendar

#1744
1920   D $85
Notebook/Calendar

#1745
1919   C+ $45
Notebook/Calendar

#1746
1939   D- $35
Notebook/Calendar

#1747
1940   D- $35
Show Program

#1748
1941   C+ $35
Guide

Reverse of #1748

#1749

1940   E $350

Promotional Book

#1750

1952   D $225

Promotional Book

#1751

1953   D $225

Promotional Book

#1752

1954   D $225

Promotional Book

#1753

1956   D $225

Promotional Book

#1754

1969   C+ $75

Promotional Book

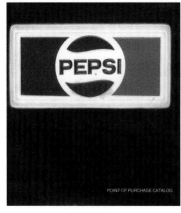

#1755

1981   B $25

Promotional Book

#1756

1987   B $25

Promotional Book

#1757

1963   B $25

Promotional Book

#1758

1936   E $200

Promotional Booklet

#1759

1938   D $200

Anniversary Booklet

#1760

1940   E $200

Promotional Booklet

#1761

1945   C+ $50

Marketing Booklet

#1762

1947   C+ $75

Set of 5 Sales Books

#1763

1956   D $150

Vending Book

#1764

1951   C+ $15

Sales Training Book

#1765

1956   B+ $5

Sales Training Booklet

#1766

1965   C+ $35

Bottler Directory

#1767
1936   E $300
36" x 24" Brochure

(Reverse of #1767)

#1768
1940   D $75
Brochure

#1769
1950   D $75
Promo Banner 22" x 34"

#1770
1950   D $75
Promo Banner 22" x 34"

#1771
1940   C+ $35
Contest Sheet 8.5" x 11"

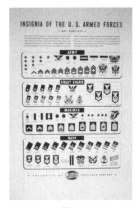

#1772
1944   D $35
Promo Flyer 8.5" x 11"

#1773

1929   D+ $150

Brochure

#1774

1936   D $125

Brochure

#1775

1945   C+ $25

Brochure

#1776

1946   C+ $25

Brochure

#1777

1945   D $150

Advertising Booklet

#1778

1949   D $85

Brochure

#1779

1940   D $50

Brochure

#1780

1951   D $65

Brochure

#1781

1960   C+ $25

Brochure

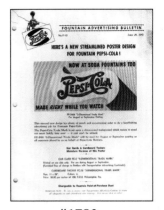

#1782

1943	D	$10

Flyer

#1783

1941	D	$10

Flyer

#1784

1949	D	$10

Flyer

#1785

1923	E	$50

Flyer

#1786

1936	D	$50

Flyer

#1787

1940	D	$50

Flyer

#1788

1939	D	$10

Flyer

#1789

1951	D	$10

Flyer

#1790

1940	D	$40

Flyer

#1791

1910 D $225

#1792

1905 E $275

#1793

1905 E $275

(Reverse of #1791)

(Reverse of #1792)

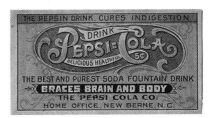

(Reverse of #1793)

#1794

1910 D $65

#1795

1909 C+ $35

#1796

1910 D $45

#1797

1910 D $65

#1798

1940 D $50

#1799

1940 D $25

#1800

1947 C+ $35

#1801

1929 D+ $50

#1802

1917	E	$50

Letter

#1803

1931	E	$25

Letter

#1804

1939	C+	$25

Legal

#1805

1941	C+	$15

Legal

#1806

1943	C+	$15

Legal

#1807

1940	D	$20

Legal

#1808

1944	C+	$15

Letter

#1809

1943	C+	$15

Letter

#1810

1948	C+	$15

Legal

#1811

1940	B	$10

Check

#1812

1940	A	$5

Check

#1813

1945	B	$10

Check

This is a very rare advertising mailer sent out by the Pepsi-Cola bottler, soliciting home sales of Pepsi-Cola. This would make a spectacular addition to any collection

#1814

1917   E $250

Advertising Mailer

(Reverse of #1814)

#1815

1936   D+ $75

Mailer

#1816

1938   D+ $35

Mailer

#1817

1939   D+ $75

Mailer

#1818

1940   D+ $125

Mailer

#1819

1958   C $5

Mailer

#1820

1955   C $5

Mailer

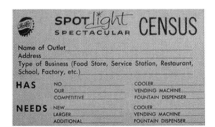

#1821

1960   B $5

Mailer

#1822

1957   C+ $5

Mailer

#1823

1965   B $5

Gift Certificate

#1824

1960   B $5

#1825

1960   C+ $15

#1826

1960   C $10

#1827

1972   C $10

#1828

1978   B $10

#1829

1980   B $5

#1830

1991   A $2

#1831

1980   A $2

Note card

#1832

1980   B $5

Wrapping Paper

#1833

1917　　E　　$500

Bradham

#1834

1915　　E　　$200

#1835

1931　　E　　$200

#1836

1930　　D+　　$100

#1837

1932　　D+　　$25

#1838

1937　　C+　　$10

#1839

1939　　C+　　$15

#1840

1941　　D　　$50

Mack

#1841

1940　　C　　$10

#1842

1940　　C+　　$10

#1843

1944　　C+　　$15

#1844

1940　　C　　$10

#1845

1947　　C　　$10

#1846

1950　　C　　$10

#1847

1951　　C　　$5

#1848

1945　　C　　$10

COLLECTING NEWSPAPER ADS

The best way to collect old Pepsi-Cola ads is to go to the library, and research the old newspapers. Once you have located the dates that the Pepsi ads appeared in, you can contact a dealer of old newspapers and order the dates you need.

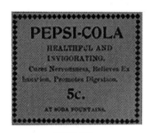

#1849

1902   D+ $20

Drop In Ad

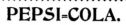

#1850

1902   D+ $20

Drop In Ad

#1851

1903   D+ $35

Drop In Ad

#1852

1907   D $45

#1853

1907   D $45

#1854

1908   D $35

#1855

1908   D $45

#1856

1909   D $45

#1857

1913   D $15

#1858

1917   D $45

#1859

1917   D $45

#1860

1919   D $45

#1861

1919   D $45

#1862

1920   D $35

#1863

1925   D $35

#1864

1929   D $25

#1865

1934   D $25

#1866

1934   D $25

#1867

1937   E $250

#1868

1939   C+ $35

#1869

1949   C+ $75

#1870

1936   C $10

#1871

1936   C $10

#1872

1936   C $10

#1873

1936   C $10

#1874

1940   C+ $35

#1875

1947   C+ $20

#1876

1939   D $30

#1877

1939   C $20

#1878

1941   C $15

#1879

1940   C $15

#1880

1940   C $15

#1881

1940   C $5

#1882

1940   C $15

#1883

1941   B $5

#1884

1942   C+ $15

#1885

1942   C $5

#1886

1940   C $5

#1887

1941   C $5

#1888

1946   C $5

#1889

1940   C $10

#1890

1945   C $5

#1891

1941   C+ $10

#1892

1942   A $3

#1893

1943   A $3

#1894

1943   C $10

#1895

1944   A $5

#1896

1945   B $5

#1897

1946   B $5

#1898

1949   B $5

#1899

1947   C $10

#1900

1947   B $5

#1901

1947   B $5

#1902

1947   B $5

#1903

1947   B $5

#1904

1951   B $5

#1905

1952   B $3

#1906

1954   A $2

#1907

1960   A $2

#1908

1960   B $5

#1909

1959   A $2

#1910

1961   A $2

#1911

1964   A $2

#1912

1967   A $2

#1913

1969   A $2

#1914

1970   B $5

#1915

1943   C $100

#1916

1951   C+ $70

#1917

1945   C+ $35

#1918

1951   C+ $25

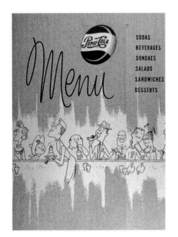

#1919

1951   C+ $20

#1920

1962   C+ $15

#1921

1945   B $15

#1922

1943   C $20

#1923

1975   A $3

#1924

1939   E $100

#1925

1940   E $100

#1926

1940   E $100

#1927

1941   D $40

#1928

1945   D $40

#1929

1956   C $20

#1930

1958   B $5

#1931

1969   A $3

#1932

1980   A $2

#1933

1908　　　E　　　$15

Convention Program

#1934

1940　　　C+　　　$75

Sheet Music

#1935

1955　　　D　　　$40

Annual Report

#1936

1943　　　D　　　$100

Annual Report

#1937

1959　　　C+　　　$25

Annual Report

#1938

1958　　　D　　　$40

Pepsi History Brochure

#1939

1960　　　B　　　$20

Pepsi History Brochure

#1940

1980　　　A　　　$15

Pepsi History Brochure

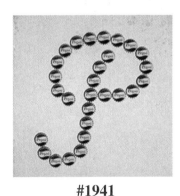

#1941

1962　　　C+　　　$15

Pepsi History Brochure

#1942

1941   C $25

Program

#1943

1973   C+ $20

Anniversary Promotion

#1944

1940   C+ $15

Music Sheet

#1945

1950   C+ $50

#1946

1950   C+ $50

#1947

1950   C+ $50

#1948

1960   C+ $5

Book Cover

#1949

1964   C+ $5

Book Cover

#1950

1964   C+ $5

Book Cover

#1951

1910   D $50

Game Board

#1952

1940   C $15

Bingo Token

#1953

1950   C+ $15

Golf Score Card

#1954

1940   C+ $15

Game

#1955

1940   C+ $65

Bridge Score Sheet

#1956

1963   B $5

Pageant Souvenir

#1957

1977   B $1

Trading Card

The trading card to the left is one of 72 trading cards given out by the Pepsi-Cola Company in 1972.

#1958

1960   C $10

Ticket Holder

#1959

1940   C $75

Bridge Pad

#1960

1960   C $2

Game Piece

#1961

1940   D+ $200

Bottle Hanger/Booklet

#1962

1940   D+ $150

Bottle Hanger

#1963

1940   D+ $50

Booklet

Each letter on these Pepsi bookmarks represents the name of a high school.

In addition to these letters shown, we also know that a number of other bookmarks exist.

#1964

1945   C $50

Bookmark

#1965

1945   D $70

Bookmark

#1966

1945   D $70

Bookmark

#1967

1956   C+ $5

Bottle Hanger

#1968

1956   C+ $5

Carton Stuffer

#1969

1960   C $5

Bottle Hanger

#1970

1960   C+ $10

Bottle Hanger

#1971

1940   B $10

Drip Bag

#1972

1940   C $45

Napkin

#1973

1951   C+ $10

Napkin

#1974

1940   C+ $15

Coaster

#1975

1940   C $10

Coaster

#1976

1960   C $10

Coaster

#1977

1940   C+ $15

Cup Lid

#1978

1960   C $10

Table Menu

#1979

1973   B $5

Table Menu

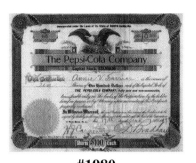

#1980

1909	E	$600

Stock Certificate

#1981

1920	E	$200

Stock Certificate

#1982

1944	C	$45

Stock Certificate

#1983

1945	C	$45

Stock Certificate

#1984

1949	C	$10

Stock Certificate

#1985

1965	C	$10

Stock Certificate

#1986

1948	D	$25

Award

#1987

1915	D	$20

Receipt

#1988

1919	D	$20

Receipt

#1989

1940	C	$10

Receipt

#1990

1955	B	$3

Receipt

#1991

1910	D	$50

Bradham Drug Prescription

#1992

1930   D $45

Grocery Reminder

#1993

1950   C+ $15

Calculator

#1994

1951   C+ $15

Mileage Chart

#1995

1940   C+ $20

Calculator

#1996

1939   E $75

Table Display 3" x 2"

#1997

1955   C+ $45

Bottle Schematic

#1998

1940   D $10

Business Card

#1999

1940   D $10

Business Card

#2000

1950   C+ $5

Business Card

#2001

1960   C $5

Business Card

#2002

1973   D $10

Skywriter Pilot Card

#2003

1964   C $10

Trading Card

#2004

1906 C+ $75

#2005

1958 C+ $10

#2006

1950 C+ $10

#2007

1943 C+ $10

#2008

1943 C+ $15

#2009

1943 B $2

#2010

1920 C+ $5

#2011

1956 B $2

#2012

1960 A $1

#2013

1956 B $2

#2014

1964 C $5

#2015

1976 C $5

#2016

1983 A $2

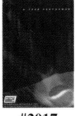

#2017

1995 A $2

#2018

1998 A $2

#2019

1903   A $100

10" x 8"

#2020

1905   D $25

8" x 10"

#2021

1908   D $25

10" x 8"

#2022

1910   D $25

10" x 8"

#2023

1939   D $25

10" x 8"

#2024

1920   D $25

10" x 8"

#2025

1950   D $25

17" x 11"

#2026

1937   D $25

14" x 11"

#2027

1950   D $25

10" x 8"

#2028

1945   A $10

Repro 14" x 11"

#2029

1941   A $10

Repro 14" x 11"

#2030

1920   A $10

Repro 14" x 11"

PEPSI-COLA COLLECTORS CLUB

Membership Application

THE PEPSI-COLA COLLECTORS CLUB is a national organization of people dedicated to the study of the history and the collecting of the memorabilia of the Pepsi-Cola Company.

THE PEPSI-COLA COLLECTORS CLUB provides:

* Nationwide and international communication among Pepsi-Cola collectors.

* Markets for buying, trading, and selling collectibles.

* Comprehensive bi-monthly newsletter.

* Annual Pepsi Fest events.

* Opportunities to buy special limited edition club commemorative items.

* Free advertising in newsletter.

If you wish to join, complete and return this form with the applicable dues for one year's membership to:

PEPSI-COLA COLLECTORS CLUB
P.O. BOX 817
CLAREMONT, CA 91711

ANNUAL DUES for primary membership in the PEPSI-COLA COLLECTORS CLUB are $18. Additional members of your family may join as associates to your primary membership for $2. per year. Associate membership is not open to friends, members of your company, or family members not living at your home or mailing address. They may join the club as a primary member, but not as an associate member under your primary membership. Associate membership does not include receiving additional copies of the PCCC newsletter, or any other official publication of the PCCC. The dues for overseas primary membership is $30 (in U.S. Funds) and includes first class postage for the monthly newsletter.

_____ $18.
Primary Member's Name (Type or Print)

_____
Street Address, Box #, Route #

_____
City, State, Zip Code

_____
Area Code - Telephone Number

_____ $2.
Associate Member's Name-Relationship

_____ $2.
Associate Member's Name-Relationship

_____ $2.
Associate Member's Name-Relationship

ML

6/02